Spaceship Earth

Spaceship Earth

BARBARA (WARD) Jackson.

Columbia University Press

NEW YORK 1966

The George B. Pegram Lectures

Reflective appraisal of the impact of science on society should be encouraged whenever possible. In addition, the transformation of traditional elements of society in an age of science is also worth examination. To these ends, the George B. Pegram Lectureship was established by the Trustees of Associated Universities, Inc. Residence at Brookhaven National Laboratory during the course of the lectures gives the lecturer opportunities for formal and informal contacts with the staff and provides a period of freedom from other duties.

As the sixth lecturer in the series, the noted English economist, Barbara Ward, elected to discuss whether modern science and technology forces us toward a more coordinated world community. What directions would world affairs take by striking new equilibria in the balance of power, balance of wealth, balance of ideologies? Miss Ward is a political scientist of world-wide stature. She has studied at the Sorbonne in Paris, in Germany, and at Somerville College, Oxford, where she took her degree in philosophy, politics, and economics. Miss Ward was an editor of *The Economist,* and counts among her publications, *The West at Bay* (1948); *A Policy for the West* (1951); *Faith and Freedom* (1954); and *The Interplay of East and West* (1957).

The Lectureship was named in honor of George B. Pegram, who worked with distinction for the nation and for Brookhaven National Laboratory in particular. Except for a few years abroad, George Pegram's entire professional career was at Columbia University, where he was a Professor of Physics, Dean, and Vice President. In 1946 he headed the Initiatory University Group which proposed that a regional center for research in the nuclear sciences be established in the New York area. Thus, he played a key role in the founding of Brookhaven and became one of the incorporating trustees of Associated Universities, Inc., remaining an active trustee for ten years.

> *Augustine O. Allen*
> *Lewis K. Dahl*
> *Edward O. Salant*
> *Thomas V. Sheehan*
> *Harold H. Smith*
> *G. B. Collins, Chairman*

Preface

In the last few decades, mankind has been overcome by the most fateful change in its entire history. Modern science and technology have created so close a network of communication, transport, economic interdependence—and potential nuclear destruction—that planet earth, on its journey through infinity, has acquired the intimacy, the fellowship, and the vulnerability of a spaceship.

In such a close community, there must be rules for survival. We have, in fact, quite a reasonable idea of what the rules might be since we live by them inside our own domestic society. We abandon the "right" to settle our disputes by force and violence and hand them over to an impartial police force and to courts of law. And, increasingly, we expect the community to see to it—through the concept of "general welfare"—that misery, grievance, and injustice do not drive us to violence. Law and welfare underpin our domestic community. These, therefore, are what we have to seek in the world at large.

But today the differences and disproportions between various parts of our world community are so great that agreed policies of cooperation run into reefs of hostility and envy. The gaps in power, the gaps in wealth, the gaps in ideology which hold the nations apart also make up the abyss into which mankind can fall to annihilation. It is on these disproportions that world policy has to concentrate—restoring a reasonable balance of power between continents, a reasonable balance of wealth between the planet's developed North and underdeveloped South, a reasonable balance of understanding and tolerance between the world's rival creeds.

Then, when the grosser inequalities have been remedied, there can be more hope of building the common institutions, policies, and beliefs which the crew of Spaceship Earth must acquire if they are to have any sure hope of survival.

BARBARA WARD

25 St. James's Street
London S.W. 1
November, 1965

Contents

Spaceship Earth

ONE

"A New History"

In our world today, all the irresistible forces of technological and scientific change are creating a single, vulnerable, human community. Yet three great disproportions—of power, of wealth, of ideology—stand in our way when we try to devise functioning worldwide institutions to civilize the vast energies of change. Until we overcome these obstacles, we are likely to be left with the energies in their raw, irrational state. And this spells disaster.

In a world that is being driven onward at apocalyptic speed by science and technology, we cannot, we must not, give up the idea that human beings can control their political and economic policies. They must have some sense of where they are trying to go, of what they are trying to do, of what the world may look like twenty years from now. It is surely inconceivable that we should turn the whole human experiment over to forces of change which we can neither master nor even fully understand. If one thing is true about the world we live in, it is that these forces are now in such spate that the physical background of our world twenty years hence will be almost completely different from what we see today. Unless, as a human society, we have some sense of direction, blind chance will take over while we shall be reduced to mounting not on our horses but on our rockets and blowing off in every direction. Such submission to chance or fate or accident neither guarantees us the best of our extraordinary and growing resources nor offers us the faintest hope of future stability. A man can go safely to sleep fishing in the middle of a quiet lake. But if he is out in the rapids, he had better reach for a paddle. If we have no sense of direction, then we shall have no sense of mastery, and if we have no sense of mastery, I doubt very much whether we shall be able to survive the enormous forces of change that sweep down upon us.

There is no need to describe in any great detail what these forces are or the degree to which the process of change is accelerating. Technology and science have become the common mode of human living and are invading every human institution and activity. The total effect is to submit the human race to a transformation more startling and complete than anything that has ever happened to it before. For any process comparable in scope and scale, we would have to go back nine or ten millennia to the invention of settled agriculture. When people stopped collecting berries and hunting for fish and meat and skins and moved on to the settled and sedentary organization of farming—tilling, sowing, weeding, and harvesting—they changed much more than their methods of work. They had to study the cycle of the seasons and begin to grasp the interactions of nature and man's activities. Care, knowledge, control, understanding lessened chance and laid the first foundations of civilization. The process lasted thousands of years and it took millennia more to work out all the potentialities of such splendid, archaic civilizations as those of Babylon or Egypt, of the Indus or the Yellow River. Change in those days was rather like the slow, steady, rising inundations of the Nile—in Andrew Marvell's words: "Vaster than empires, and more slow."

But today, suddenly, the experience of the human race is much more like that of being put in a barrel and sent over Niagara Falls. It is not simply that change is infinitely more drastic and affects everything we do. It is also occurring at a speed which is geared to none of the old speeds—of years, seasons, lifetimes, generations. Now it is hardly even geared to the flash of human intelligence. It is computer speed, accomplishing the 500-year work of 500 scientists in five minutes.

This accelerating process will, I believe, be checked by no traditional attitudes or institutions since its methods, quite apart from its aims, are essentially revolutionary. We cannot study, analyze, check, and compare without modifying the object of our studies.

Take the most primitive people we can choose—say, the bushmen of the Kalahari Desert. In one sense they are not primitive—if primitive means ignorant. By becoming the most extraordinary observers of natural things, they know more about the behavior of plant and animal than, perhaps, the most trained modern zoologist. But if we go to the bushmen these days, what do we find? We find anthropologists and zoologists studying them. So, inevitably, their way of life is on the way out. Even if a tribe is primitive now, it is probably being studied to a pitch that stops it being primitive in short order. The older people become self-conscious; the younger ones want to train as anthropologists. There is thus a unique

pervasiveness about our new habits of scientific and technological thought and practice which no one can evade. Cultures
and societies, like watches, are rarely the same when they have
been taken to pieces. This, essentially, is what our new methods of analysis and comparison entail. Quite apart from common tools and methods, we also have mental attitudes that do
not vary from culture to culture and are common to a single
world civilization.

This is only one example among many of our underlying
trend towards unity. I need not underline the conquest of
space. Whatever the delays, we shall have supersonic planes
and I—alas—will probably fly in one, reaching London from
New York before breakfast, having left after breakfast. Total,
worldwide, communication is also nearly a fact. With
Early Bird we are almost a world society of village gossips. In
1963—if I may be allowed a brief illustration—my husband
was on one of his journeys for the United Nations Special
Fund. He went, as I recall it, to India, Malaysia, Ethiopia,
Liberia, and Ghana. When he reached home, I said: "Lovely
to see you, dear. Tell me about it. How is development getting
along? What are they talking about?" His reply was: "Chris-
tine Keeler." There you have the village gossip.

But the issue is much more serious. This extension of all our
senses by electronic means of communication creates a world
awareness of what is going on in our planetary society, and
this is bound to become a new factor in the pressures at work
in world politics. I very much doubt whether, even five years
ago, the scale of the world's grief at the death of Pope John
and the world's shocked horror at the death of President
Kennedy would have been even conceivable. The new means

of instant communication did, in a strange way, give people the feeling that they were taking personal part in a tragic, worldwide wake.

I was in Northern Rhodesia when the news of the appalling tragedy in Dallas came through, and there Kenneth Kaunda, who is now president of this new country, was about to address a large political meeting. When the news reached him, he broke off the proceedings to lead his large African audience in a prayer and a hymn. Within hours, it was possible for remote cities—Accra, Lagos, Monrovia—to watch the raw grief and stunned shock of the American people. Within days, millions followed "the captains and the kings" along the funeral route. We do not yet know the full consequences of this instantaneous transmission of human emotions, reactions, and needs across all the physical barriers of our planet. But we know enough to guess that it will enormously strengthen the sense of nearness and human proximity—not always for good, for who loves all his neighbors?—but always for awareness, and always for attention, for influence, and concern.

Now let me take another factor of unity—the underlying resemblances of the modern economic system. I am not talking about the interconnections of markets and trade and investment on a worldwide scale. We will turn to them later. Here I would like to pick up something more profound—the degree to which certain necessities in the whole process of modernization tend to produce similar structures and policies all round the world—and to do so without any regard to differing political and social philosophies.

The transformation of man's productive system by capital and technology began in the West at the end of the eighteenth century within the framework of private property and the competitive market. But after a hundred years or so, the private element has been supplemented by a whole range of governmental powers. No one planned this development. As we shall see, it has been almost a byproduct of a single, overwhelming, human activity—war. But the fact that it has been the consequence of practice, not of dogma, shows the degree to which it is a reflection not so much of human foresight as of technological necessity.

At the outset of the modern economy—in Britain—a number of separate entrepreneurs worked for profit and, by reinvesting the profit, created the capital they needed for further advance. But most early economists were not too optimistic about the continued development and expansion of this new system. They feared that as resources were used up and became scarcer and as the available labor supply was absorbed, thus pushing up wages, the entrepreneur's essential profits would be squeezed out and he would therefore cease to invest. If he did so, the whole dynamic expansion of the system would come to an end since the only people capable of making expansive decisions would have ceased to make them. Nor did there seem to be alternative centers of decision-making. Economists either did not believe in the competence of government to pursue effective policies after the incompetence and corruption of state-run mercantilism, or—with Marx—they thought the state simply reflected business interests and would not intervene on ideological grounds. This underlying pessimism is one reason why, in the early nineteenth century, economics was named "the dismal science."

Yet in spite of temporary, though regular, crises of stagnation—the down-turns of the trade cycle—and in spite of a depression of catastrophic proportions in the 1930s, the prophets of doom have been disproved by the behavior of the market economy. They reckoned without the impact of man's oldest and least reputable occupation—war. War did two things. It accelerated tremendously the speed and range of inventions and hence the productivity of the new technology. Think of the impact of naval warfare on the elaboration of the lighter metals needed to make weapons that ships could carry without sinking. Think of the expansion of grain production with a reduced labor force in two world wars. Think of tanks into tractors. Think of the forced-draft development of the car, the aircraft, the rocket, under the insistent demands of war. Think, above all, of nuclear energy. All these tremendous breakthroughs were speeded up a thousand times by the frantic search for victory.

The second modification introduced by war was the realization that private consumption and production to satisfy it are not the only sources of effective demand. Government also has a part to play. Government orders and government expenditure did, of course, play some part in the traditional Western economy. But the assumption, broadly speaking, was that government would secure its own purchasing power—through taxation—out of the wealth already created by the private economy. There was little belief that the government might, by its own direct intervention, take decisions which expanded the whole base of the economy and thus added to the total sum of wealth available to the community. The pioneering British had little confidence in government. Their economy had emerged from a period of clumsy governmental interventions and inefficient governmental monopolies, and early economists wanted only to free the market from the dead hand of Whitehall and the "Circumlocution Office."

Yet throughout the nineteenth century, as the scale and mechanization of war increased, government orders in time of war hastened the expansion of heavy industry. In World War I, such developments as the setting up of the Ministry of Munitions in Britain was a revelation of how to speed up heavy industrial growth. In World War II, the United States doubled its industrial capacity between 1940 and 1944, adding in four short years the equivalent growth of over a century. Such massive interventions, creating wholly new levels of capacity and output, were not financed only by withdrawing wealth, via taxation, from the existing private economy. In most ways, they were simply additions. They built, at the cost, admittedly, of some inflation, almost a completely new wealth-producing apparatus on top of the old. Civilian demand, held back by shortages and forced saving during the war, surged forward afterwards to take advantage of the new facilities and, as a result, the war which was the ruin of some countries led, in others, to undreamed-of levels of new wealth.

These two war-based experiences—of a vast acceleration of technical sophistication and of the effectiveness of government decisions to expand the economy—effectively broke the gloomy trap of the earlier economists. Rising productivity springing from new energy, new materials, new techniques rose sharply and steadily enough for profits and wages to rise together—the wages helping to provide the mass market in which profits—*à la* Henry Ford—could be earned by a small return on a vast turnover.

And the effectiveness of government intervention to increase capacity in time of war led inescapably to the conclusion that government could also intervene effectively to ensure that the economy did not fall away into depression in peace time but would maintain, on the contrary, a steady rate of expansion. At first, this new responsibility of government took such forms as the Congressional Act of 1946, bidding the government to prevent unemployment. But in the last two decades, the responsibility has been more clearly defined as the government's duty to see that total demand in the economy is such as to employ all its resources and to maintain their upward expansion. Not wild radical thinkers but such formidably respectable economists as the official consultants of the Organization for Economic Cooperation and Development (the OECD) now state without hesitation that the secret of economic stability and growth lies in the steady maintenance of demand, and it is one of the government's responsibilities to see that the balance is kept.

Thus, not by theory or dogma but largely by war-induced experience, the Western market economies have come to accept the effectiveness and usefulness of a partnership between public and private activity. The government has its essential part to play in keeping demand stable and ensuring an upward movement in the whole economy. Sometimes the stimulus to sufficient demand will come from an unbalanced budget or higher public spending on public needs, sometimes from a tax cut which increases private purchasing power. But there is now no question of exclusive reliance on any one instrument or any one method. The pragmatic market economies have worked out their own evolving combinations of public and private responsibility and the result is the dynamic but surprisingly stable mixed economy of the Western world.

Meanwhile changes which may ultimately prove as far-reaching are taking place on the Soviet side. In some ways, of course, change is more difficult for the Communists. On the whole, Western nations are not too much given to dogma. We have a few enthusiasts who refuse to pay federal taxes because of the encroachment of "big government." America employs perhaps rather more jargon than Europe on the issue of "creeping socialism" and Communist plots to induce inflation and national bankruptcy. But, on the whole, in economics the Western world can move from position to position with little sense of contradiction and incompatibility. We had no very fixed views before so we do not have to bother too much about what we believe now. It is a considerable source of strength.

The unfortunate Russians, on the contrary, set out to build a modern economy on the basis of strict doctrine. This doctrine demanded that all economic decisions be made by the State. They were not pushed into this by the chance effectiveness of war. In a queer way, they were not even pushed into it by Marx, who believed that in a classless society, the State would "wither away." But if a doctrine demands the abolition of all private entrepreneurs—the prime movers and decision-makers in the Western experiment—you are really only left with public entrepreneurs, in other words, the government and its civil servants.

Now, the early decisions in Soviet Russia may not have been too difficult for public authorities to take. They mainly covered the kind of decisions Western governments make in war—a massive increase in all the capital components of heavy industry and all the services needed to support industrialization. (The Soviet planners also made brilliantly successful decisions in another area in which, in the West too, the role of the State is paramount—the field of education.) The first Five Year Plans for industry underlined the effectiveness of what one might call "war planning." Indeed, they enabled the Russians to resist one of the most overwhelming armed attacks in history. In those first decades, only in agriculture were the hints beginning that a command system, based on rigid planning from the center, might contain its own "internal contradictions" and require reforms of structure as drastic as anything the Communists postulate for private enterprise.

Today, the retreat from total central state decision has become a dominant fact in Soviet and Eastern European economics. The reasons behind it stem from the inability of planned quotas of resources, planned wages, planned prices, and planned returns to produce the variety and quality of goods the consumer in Communist countries is beginning to demand. In central planning and accounting, a badly made television set fulfills the factory's quota just as well as a well-made one. Dresses which fit dwarfs, or shoes for two left feet still satisfy norms fixed by weight or number. So, in order to produce goods which consumers really want, the Soviet world is beginning a variety of experiments all of which tend towards the procedures of the decentralized market economy.

Spurred on by Professor Liberman's advocacy of profits as a guide to efficiency, the Russians have allowed a wide range of factories producing consumer goods to make their own arrangements with retailers, fix their own prices and profit margins, and share their own bonuses. The Czechs are experiment-

ing with prices that rise or fall according to demand. The Poles
are handing down some planning and price-fixing functions to
groups of manufacturers. The Yugoslavs have gone further
than anybody, not only leaving factories to fix their own prices
and earn their own profits but bringing in Western goods to
compete with local products and thus establish external standards of efficiency and competence.

So the outcome of years of experiment in the processes of
industrialization has been to lead the market economies towards planning and the planned economies toward the market.
Of the two, the restoration of the market in the Soviet sphere is
perhaps the most remarkable since, as I have already pointed
out, a freight of doctrine has had to be shed in the process.
Ultimately one can perhaps hope that the new attention to the
consumer in market terms may have some effect on the "consumer" or voter in terms of politics. But for the present it is
surprising enough, in view of Marxist dogma, to see commissars getting down to the problem of interest rates and
possibly even saying: "Comrade Ivanovitch, your rate of profit
has been very low these last six months. Go to Siberia!"

I have dwelt at some length on this remarkable reversal of
traditional attitudes—in both West and East—not simply because it is a fascinating commentary on the supposed immuta-
bility of doctrine and the actual influence of need and fact. It
is more than fascinating. It is highly significant. It suggests
that whatever the starting point a nation may adopt in the application of science and technology, through savings, the
processes of production, it is likely at some point to produce a
version of mixed economy. It therefore suggests—as do our
experiences in transport or communication—that in this new

world order of technological and scientific change, the forces leading towards a certain unity of human experience are stronger than the forces leading to increasing difference and division.

Now I do not mean by this example to suggest that ideas and beliefs are not important. We shall be looking at them later. But the economic example I have chosen illustrates the likelihood that a certain inner logic in the deployment of our new technological tools leads to remarkable resemblances of organization and practice even in societies which think of themselves as widely or totally divergent.

One can think of other examples. The pattern of the birth rate is one. As nations begin to modernize, one of the early consequences—in democratic India as in Communist China —is a spurt in the growth of population. Even more striking is the worldwide acceleration in urban growth. All round the world, in developed or developing societies, in planned or market economies, the same irresistible movement to the cities goes on. If world population on the average is growing by 2 percent a year, cities grow by 4 percent, the great megalopolitan areas by 8 percent. Moscow grows as quickly as Paris, Rio de Janeiro as Chicago. It is a gloomy footnote to this common experience that virtually all the urban patterns that result are equally inhospitable to the human race—but this, again, only underlines the degree to which the impact of modernizing science and technology is creating a common experience, common dilemmas, common mistakes, and, more hopefully, common opportunities for the entire human race.

The last of these overriding resemblances is both the most obvious and the most fateful. For the first time in human his-

tory, a nation can lob a little device over a neighbor's back-
yard and blow him up and everything else with it. If this fact
does not create a "community," I do not know what can. If we
can all be destroyed, together, in two or three acts of grandilo-
quent incineration, then we are neighbors.

In short, we have become a single human community. Most
of the energies of our society tend towards unity—the energy
of science and technological change, the energy of curiosity
and research, of self-interest and economics, the energy—in
many ways the most violent of them all—the energy of potential aggression and destruction. We have become neighbors in
terms of inescapable physical proximity and instant communication. We are neighbors in economic interest and technological direction. We are neighbors in facets of our industrialization and in the pattern of our urbanization. Above all, we are
neighbors in the risk of total destruction. The atomic bomb
would rain down on the just and unjust, on the Communist
and the non-Communist, on the slave and the free, and could
leave us all with our last appalling unity—the unity of annihilation.

The society of man has never before been in this position.
Individual societies have succumbed. I suppose one could
argue that our remoter human ancestors before the second Ice
Age would have faced the same risk of annihilation if they had
not taken shelter in the caves in which they drew their remarkable pictures of animals—how strange it is, after perhaps a
hundred millennia, to come back to the possibility that we may
need to retreat once more into caves in order to survive. But I
can think of no other analogy. In the past, whatever the
horrors of war, other societies in other regions would be sure to

carry on. Now, it seems, we have reached a planetary point of no return.

In fact, I can think of only one way of expressing the degree to which interdependence and community have become the destiny of modern man. I borrow the comparison from Professor Buckminster Fuller, who, more clearly than most scientists and innovators, has grasped the implications of our revolutionary technology. The most rational way of considering the whole human race today is to see it as the ship's crew of a single spaceship on which all of us, with a remarkable combination of security and vulnerability, are making our pilgrimage through infinity. Our planet is not much more than the capsule within which we have to live as human beings if we are to survive the vast space voyage upon which we have been engaged for hundreds of millennia—but without yet noticing our condition. This space voyage is totally precarious. We depend upon a little envelope of soil and a rather larger envelope of atmosphere for life itself. And both can be contaminated and destroyed. Think what could happen if somebody were to get mad or drunk in a submarine and run for the controls. If some member of the human race gets dead drunk on board our spaceship, we are all in trouble. This is how we have to think of ourselves. We are a ship's company on a small ship. Rational behavior is the condition of survival.

Rational rules of behavior are what we largely lack. The drives and energies that have built our world society have been, on the whole, the energies of power and wealth and enmity. We seem to lack any comparable energy in building the institutions, the laws, the habits, the traditions which express our moral and social purposes—obligation, equality, dignity, respect, neighborliness in its fullest sense which means, if we have not too much debased the word, the sense and practice of brotherly love.

Thus the human race, to which we all belong, is in a strained, unbalanced condition. Our physical unity has gone far ahead of our moral unity. Our inability to do anything but live together physically is not matched by any of the institutions that would enable us to live together decently. When, therefore, I talk about a "sense of direction," what I chiefly have in mind is our chance of bridging this extraordinary and sinister gap. Can we prevent the sheer inventions and pressures of our society from running so far beyond our political, social, and moral wisdom? Can we take some of the energy and imagination, some of the vision and hard work that are forcing us together in so many fields and use them, at the higher levels of social and political organization, to build the institutions of a decent human society? Can we turn the mob into a community? Can we convert casual physical proximity into the city of man?

The plain truth is that if we cannot, as a human community, create the institutions of civilized living, our chances of carrying on the human experiment are just about nil. This is no longer hyperbole; it is no longer rhetoric or cliche; it is simple fact. Admittedly, to invent institutions or create a community is much more difficult than simply to drift with the physical and technological movements of world change. Man is much less malleable than the atom. He has unpredictable ideas and reactions. He is attached to old institutions and distrustful of new ones—we cannot feed his prejudices into a cyclotron and conveniently smash them up. We cannot put him into an accelerator, however much the world may need to speed up the processes of institution-building.

Yet I do not think we should be too much discouraged. The human record is not simply "nasty, brutish, and short." We have produced more than wars and violence. In fact, we have a pretty good idea of the kind of institutions men need in order to live in peace for, over long periods and wide areas, we have in fact done so within domestic society.

The essence of civil peace is the sacrifice of private force. The citizen abandons to law courts, to impartial police, to all manner of mediating bodies—of arbitration, of conciliation—the right to settle his disputes. Increasingly, he asks society in return—through his government—to see that his economic and social grievances are not such as to leave him in urgent and unsatisfied need of redress. Most of the tasks of government come under these two headings—of law and order on the one hand, of welfare on the other. And the essence of our international anarchy today is that the functions of order and most of the functions of welfare still stop at the arbitrary boundaries of states. The greatest institutional gap in our world is created by an inescapable, planetary, interdependence which breeds common grievances and creates common needs and opportunities, yet is matched by virtually no instruments of worldwide order and welfare. And it is through this gap that mankind can tumble into annihilation.

If we take the provision of security and of some measure of welfare as these minimum tasks of government, they should not be beyond the capacity of a worldwide society. Some will bring up at this point the objection of the scale. It is all very well to talk about the tasks of government when nations alone are in question. But the three billion inhabitants of the globe are another matter. Effective institutions to guarantee peace will simply be swamped by numbers.

But this criticism overlooks the history of the Chinese. They have always made up a quarter of the human race and, as the human race increases, up go the Chinese as well. It is almost as though they could not fail to be this 25 percent. Today, with some additions and some subtractions, they still live under a system that bears a family resemblance to their organization over the last two thousand years. In fact, one of the most fruitful ways of looking at the regime of Mao Tse-tung may well be to think of him as the founder of a new dynasty, in succession to the long line of Ching and Ming and Sung and Tang. He resembles one of those peasant leaders who, in the past, have sometimes rescued China from the worst of its crises. Such leaders do not usually disturb the bureaucracy— Confucian mandarins then, Marxist commissars now (possibly Marxo-Confucians tomorrow?)—and one or two of them experimented very boldly in land reform and in the nationalization of industry and trade. Thus the belief that government can intervene sharply in the processes of an economy is not new in Chinese history. One can even argue that the old sense of the emperor as the source and guarantee of well-being in the nation's life has reappeared in Mao's astonishing cult of personality. In earlier times, the emperor's virtue made the harvests prosper. Now to read Mao's works makes you world champion at table tennis. There is a link between the two moods.

But this is by the way. The important fact about the tradi-

tional Chinese system was the fact that for over two millennia
—the longest endurance of a state system in human history—a
quarter of the human race lived, with only relatively brief in-
terruptions, under common institutions. The starting point was
the abandonment of anarchic, competitive feudalism and the
setting up, some centuries before Christ, of a centralized government under the Han dynasty. The old states became prov-
inces and in fact carried on most of their affairs in the old way
according to their own traditions and customs. But the central
government fulfilled enough of the functions of order and welfare to create a coherent system of political stability. The emperor was responsible for external security and had some over-
sight over trade routes and communications. In times of fam-
ine, the government undertook public works and oversaw
grain distribution. The later dynasties introduced large-scale
irrigation. True, these are, if you like, minimum functions of
central government. But they were enough to underpin the
system.

Now, if common institutions held together a quarter of the
human race for over two thousand years, we can hardly argue
that the task of government becomes *a priori* impossible simply because the remaining three-quarters are added. If fairly
minimal safeguards of security and order and minimum interventions to enhance welfare—coupled, of course, with a certain sense of common purpose and loyalty—have been enough
to give an orderly civil society to a quarter of all the globe's
inhabitants, we cannot be sure, especially in the light of modern transport and communication, that multiplying the number
of citizens by four rules out the hope of a wider experiment.
The remarkable point about the Chinese system was how small

the centralized functions needed to be. The bulk of people's daily lives were controlled and organized at the provincial and, indeed, at the village level. Central government undertook no more than the minimum functions necessary to create an organized peaceful society. True, this is one of the features of the Chinese system the Communists are changing drastically, but it remained true for two millennia and suggests that a world system could be minimal—which clearly it needs to be—yet effective and enduring.

But one can question whether the issue of numbers is the crucial one. China simply proves, so runs the argument, that a very large number of people can be organized under a despotism. But this is surely not the pattern proposed for the future of the human race. Yet if you introduce the principle of civil liberty, of choice, of elected government, the task of world order becomes inconceivably complicated. On what possible basis could choices be made, parties organized, leaders picked, elections conducted? Even if one admits that a world system is conceivable on some authoritarian basis, free-wheeling, unpredictable, chancey, disorderly democratic processes are simply too much to swallow.

Yet here again history is not so pessimistic. When the Greeks introduced elective, legal government and felt the chief difference between themselves and the powerful and splendid despotisms next door to lie simply in the fact that they, as Greek citizens, lived under laws of their own making, they did not believe the scale of free government could grow much beyond the city state. The colonization of Athens took the form not of extending Attica's control but founding daughter cities. Indeed, some historians argue that the whole effort to unite or

federate the Greek city-states in face of the Persian threat
failed because the Athenians could not bear to give up the
loved and limited authority of the *polis.*

Yet an essential part of the political history which the Greek
experience helped to foster in the West has been the steady extension in scale and space of legal, representative government.
Italian city-states, Britain's constitutional monarchy, the continental federation of the United States—these are stages along
the way towards an ever greater extension of the "open society." Today one can add the vast, continental, plural democracy of India in which the electorate alone is greater than
America's inhabitants. If such extensions have already proved
possible, we cannot, once again, lose faith on *a priori* grounds
in the possibility of further growth. If a free continent is possible, why not an association of free continents? History does not
tell us that this is a pipe dream. If all our physical and technological energies, drives, discoveries, and proximities demand
common institutions on a planetary scale, nothing in mankind's
past behavior suggests that the goal is inherently impossible.

Not impossible—and yet, we must admit, it is a task which
confronts us with incredible complexity and obstruction. In the
past, the great majority of citizens were relatively passive.
Most of them, like the Chinese, tended in normal times to accept kings and dynasties as they would the forces of nature.
Empires rose and fell, conquerors triumphed and failed, but
life in the villages went on unchanged. The enormous disproportion between the power, the wealth, and often the outlook
of the few families at the apex of society and the very modest
opportunities of the mass of the people hardly entered into the

political equation. When, after the Renaissance and the Refor-
mation, the majority of citizens in the Western world began to
demand political rights, economic opportunity, and a mind of
their own, the vigorous rise of the middle classes was already
in motion, reducing the old disparities and, by the early nineteenth century, a fervid spirit of nationalism created a sense of
common direction and purpose to hold the community together. It was, if you like, the old tribalism writ large, but it
blanketed inequalities and provided a mystique for the "common good."

In our world society, neither the old passivities nor the new
energies can be relied on. The world will not accept the
dominance of a few "top nations." Yet the disparities in power,
in wealth, in outlook and ideology are so great that the creation of some kind of working community in the Western manner also seems to be ruled out. The analogies between an ultimate world order and the experience either of despotic states
of the size of China or of democratic communities on the
American or Indian continental scale are thus not wholly convincing. In theory, no doubt, they point towards the possibility
of a world community. In practice, the disparities seem too
great. If mankind is to achieve political, social, and moral institutions to match his economic and technological drives, the
disparities must be lessened. Unbalanced power, dispropor-
tionate wealth, the ideological abyss—these are the obstacles
to world order. These are, therefore, in the same measure obstacles to the survival of man.

TWO

The Balance of Power

Our only worldwide organization—in intent if not in practice —tells us that we are a world of nations. "The United Nations" enshrines the principle of international order. Since, however, it specifically admits the absolute sovereignty of nations, it rather resembles the compliment that hypocrisy pays to virtue. It is *not* fully a world organization. It does *not* transcend nationalism. But at least the existence of such an organ shows that the human race feels in some obscure way that it ought to try.

Some people would argue that the U.N. is hardly even an association of "nations" since the word is being stretched to almost impossible limits to cover communities with remarkably little in common. Between the nearly 200 million inhabitants, with per capita incomes of over $2,500, of the United States and the 600,000 seminomads of Mauretania, are there any resemblances which justify the use of a common term to describe them? Between the 700 millions or more of continental China, "*le grand absent*," and the 300,000 islanders perched on the rocks of Malta? Or Russia's rising quarter-billion and the million or so Albanians who so rudely reject its leadership?

What we have in fact is not so much nations as an extraordinary spectrum of political communities. The largest are the continental empires which have spread by settlement or conquest or both over adjacent areas of land inhabited by weaker peoples—or not much inhabited at all. China and the United States are such giants and so is Russia—provided, as seems likely today, it can finally incorporate its Asian peoples into an unbreakable community. India, made a single state only by cultural unity and external conquest, is possibly a giant for the future. But it could also become a continent of separate linguistic or "nation states."

Europe is *par excellence* the continent of nations. Here language and frontier came to coincide in Western Europe at the end of the Middle Ages just as the rise of the middle classes brought, on the one hand, commercial growth and rivalry between national markets, and, on the other, a democratic demand to participate in government and therefore to understand its language. It was a chance coincidence but an incredibly powerful invention. The nationally conscious, economically competitive states—Portugal, Spain, France, Holland, Britain—set off round the world, carrying ideas and rivalry with them. They established the commercial empires, fighting each other every step of the way, took nationalism to the Americas (Latin America, as a result, is a continent of nation-states), brought ideals of self-government and hence of nationalism to Asia and later to Africa, and produced, ultimately, a worldwide commitment to the ideal of self-determination as the basic right to be enjoyed by man's collective communities. This right has, in the last twenty years, ended seaborne colonialism and brought over fifty new nations into the United Nations.

But, of course, they are not nations, or not yet. For language and frontier to coincide in human affairs is the exception and, before the coming of any demand for popular participation, not very important. In the old empires and dynasties, peasants expected the language of their rulers to be different. One had to go down to the tribe for the coincidence of tongue and territory. In places like New Guinea one had to go down to the village itself. But few tribes outside Europe had, until recently, gone through the processes of consolidation and common political experience which had made Anglo-Saxons and Danes and Celts and Normans into Englishmen or Gauls and Norsemen into the French. "National self-determination," for instance, even in Eastern Europe in the early twentieth century, produced states with angry minorities speaking different tongues. Nation-building still continues there, underneath the Communist surface. Similarly, in many parts of Asia and everywhere in post-colonial Africa, you have states trying to become nations, trying to overcome the divisions and distractions of tribal differences, trying to work out a common language, trying to create, by party loyalty or by loyalty to the leader, the sense of cohesion and participation which nationalism gives in Europe.

And below these new post-colonial states are scraps and leavings of the processes of de-colonization—islands so remote, territories so poor, areas so uninhabited that they either make virtually resourceless states—like some of the territories on the fringe of the African deserts—or have little choice but to remain dependencies. One thinks of Mauritius or the Seychelles or France's *departements* in the Antilles. Thus, between the top of the ladder of states—where Russia or the United States dwells in irresistible might—and the tiny fragments at the bottom, the disproportions of power are so great that they create, almost of themselves, hazards to stability and survival. A chicken is not safe in the proximity of an elephant, even of a benevolent elephant. And not all the elephants are benevolent. Or rather, their views of benevolence do not always look so convincing at the level of the chicken. The Soviet elephant may still believe that only Communist chickens lead a full and decent life. The American elephant may see no difficulty in owning 80 percent of the chicken's nascent industrial structure. But there *is* a chicken's point of view and if it is totally—and benevolently—disregarded by the elephants, the chicken may be tempted to ask one of the elephants to get the other one out. Then there is very little left of the chicken.

It is not simply scale that provides such enormous variations and uncertainties. We are yet very far from knowing whether the present spectrum will last. Are we clear that the Russian and Indian giants have taken their final form? Is Europe not possibly entering a post-national phase? Are not many of the new micro states aware of their extraordinary weakness and anxious to lessen it in association with neighbors? A tremor of constitution-making and constitution-breaking runs over most of the world today and both the efforts to create different units of sovereignty—in Europe, in East Africa, in Central America, in Malaysia—and the extreme difficulty of doing so underline the instability of state structures in this early post-colonial phase.

I feel certain myself that a whole range of intermediate political institutions between the family at one end of the scale and any ultimate world authority at the other is here to stay.

World institutions will need to be mediated to ordinary citizens through secondary authorities just as the Chinese emperor's control was exercised most of the time through provincial officers. The United States, China at one level of magnitude, France, Britain at another, Uruguay, Ceylon at another—all these are self-conscious, highly articulated, historical communities with the stuff of survival in them. But even if they are lasting building blocks of world order, they may enter into new associations. After all, the family, too, is a basic human institution, but it takes many different forms—clans, extended families, monogamy, concurrent polygamy, and, that worst of all patterns, the consecutive polygamy of the Western world— worst, I mean, for the least offending of the parties, the children.

But to return to the survival of states and nations, they can, I think, be judged to be among the likely building blocks of ultimate world order. Equally one can judge them, in their present shape, to be the building blocks of present world *disorder*. For if one tries to analyze what they have in common, ultimately one comes back to only one thing—their claim to sovereignty. In fact, the only way to define all these communities clustered along the ladder of size, from China at the top to Chad or Gabon at the bottom, is to point to the single fact that puts them on the same ladder at all. This is their claim to sovereignty—to absolute loyalty from their own citizens and absolute freedom of action towards everyone else's. They are, each, a point of ultimate authority and a focus of ultimate loyalty. Put in this way, the claim to absolute sovereignty looks as ridiculous as in fact it is. It is patently ridiculous for Chad since even its budget has to be directly subsidized from Paris.

But it is, finally, just as ridiculous for China since, among the ultimate decisions which are *not* under its own control, is whether it will be bombed into nuclear annihilation. And if you cannot choose to survive, your subsidiary freedoms of action somehow look a little secondary. The United States is, of course, in roughly the same case.

This exclusive focus of authority and loyalty within the state is not an abstract thing. It is composed of men enjoying the most intoxicating occupation offered to mankind—the exercise of power. Absolute power may "corrupt absolutely" but nothing exercises the same almost hypnotic appeal. To see the serried ranks and the awed faces, to issue the defiances and hurl the insults—how it appeals to the insecure and fearful side of man. To take the wise decisions and feel the full responsibility for correct action—how it appeals to him under his confident and benevolent aspect. Government is an all but irresistible intoxication and the desire to exercise it and therefore preserve it at the highest level—which today is the *state* level —is an overwhelming temptation. But it is also a sham.

We will look at the economic limitations on effective sovereignty later. If even a state on the scale of Russia cannot feed itself, if the United States is not entirely in control of its balance of payments, how can one measure the economic limitations of the micro-states? Their limits must be seen to be almost as total as the sovereignty they claim. But economics are secondary. Survival comes first. The present organization of mankind in a lawless assembly of competing sovereignties deprives every state of security, great and small alike. If the justification of the sovereignty claimed for the state is that it secures safety and well-being for the ordinary citizen—and what other justification can there be?—then our objective judgment must be clear. Undiluted national sovereignty is no longer an efficient or sufficient instrument of government.

The risks are clearly greatest for the smaller states, and we will begin with them. In theory, at least, the prospects of small communities have improved in the twentieth century. Throughout history, they have been at the mercy of powerful neighbors. To be incorporated in the imperial system or sphere of influence of some larger state has been the lot of most small groups in the past. Their only safeguard lay in the degree to which their subjection made little difference to their quiet agricultural or pastoral pursuits. Not all empires were reforming or proselytizing empires. Most of them left their humblest subjects alone. The peasants of North India passed from Guptas to Mauryas to Rajputs to Mughals to British without altering their Hindu gods. But the processes of conquest, nonetheless, were full of rapine and violence and, whenever an old imperial order began to collapse and new pressures thrust in from elsewhere to take its place, the communities entered into what Arnold Toynbee has called "times of troubles"—the violent, unstable, interlude between the ending of one period of imperial order and the coming of the next.

But in the twentieth century, something unprecedented has begun in the human record. The concept of human rights has been extended to cover the rights of human communities, and among those rights is "self-determination" which, crudely put, is the right not to have a more powerful neighbor sit on your

head simply because you are small and he is big. In other
words, officially imperialism is no longer a legitimate way of
running human affairs.

Stop to think for a moment what a startling change this is.
For millennia, from the very beginning of human records, the
rule has been that might is right, that if you are large enough
to hold down your neighbors and exploit them, you can use
them, take their territory, and oppress them at will. It is not, I
think, in any way an accident that the Wilsonian doctrine
of the self-determination of peoples was formulated by a
democratic society in the United States. Individual democratic
rights demand to be extended to individuals living in community, in other words, to the nation. You cannot free a man as a
person and oppress him as a citizen. A world half slave, half
free, is as inconsistent and self-contradictory as a society run
on the same lines. Thus the incorporation of the right of
human communities, small as well as great, to respect, dignity,
and self-determination must be reckoned a genuine element of
progress in human affairs.

It is the justification, if you like, for the voting systems of the
United Nations which takes no account of the ridiculous disproportions between the size of different states. The fact that
Mauretania with 600,000 people has the same vote as the
United States with rising 200 million people has its rationale in
the theory of equal respect for small entities. Inside the state,
an unemployed automobile worker is almost as remote from
the influence, standing, and effectiveness of Henry Ford as
Mauretania from the United States. But in democratic society,
we give both of them the same vote to even up the influence,
or rather, the noninfluence of the little man. In the United Na-

tions, under a similar theory, the equal vote of Jamaica and the Soviet Union expresses the world's respect for Jamaica's status and Jamaica's right not to be "pushed about." It does not, any more than the single vote of John Doe on relief in Detroit, suggest equality of influence, choice, decision, or effectiveness with the magnates whether they run the automobile industry or half the globe.

The theory is undoubtedly a big step forward. Mankind is most unlikely to rectify situations which it does not consider to be wrong and in spite of the fact that the weakness of small neighbors and the predatory instincts of large powers have been the greatest single cause of war, it is really not until this century that we even envisaged a different ordering of society —one in which might was not right and, among states as among men, the "poorest state hath a right to live as the richest"—to adapt John Lilburne's pregnant phrase. But the theory is still very far from the practice. Today practice faces just the kind of interregnum of empire which, in the past, has been most productive of disorder and violence.

In twenty short years, the whole system of European colonial control has been dismantled with unprecedented speed. A host of new nations, many of them divided and insecure, has been created in the interstices of the Great Powers. The new dispensation may be final. Under the new principle of the U.N.—that of self-determination—it ought to be. But can we be sure? Here the disproportion in scale between the powers becomes an added cause of insecurity.

Let us for a moment look at the historical experience of what one could call, by analogy with broadcasting, the "mush areas" of the world. "Mush areas" are places where the signals given by major transmitters meet and blur. They are a sort of no-man's-land in which no one signal, and therefore no one authority or system of communication, is established. There is blurring, competition, out-shouting, and a growing determination to throw the other rascals out.

In Western history, the Balkans have become the classical example of a "mush area." As the old Turkish empire crumbled and its signals in Bulgaria and Serbia and Walachia and Bessarabia grew weaker, two rival imperial systems—the Russian on the one hand and Austria-Hungary, increasingly backed by Germany, on the other—jostled to set up their own predominance. Every local Balkan shift of power or dynasty or even sympathy threatened one or other of the rival external imperialisms and each maneuvred, through local puppets, to get the other out. This was the essence of the recurrent "Eastern Question" in the second half of the nineteenth century.

In the twentieth it proved irresistible. The European Powers came to compromise agreements everywhere else—in Persia, in the Far East, in Africa. But the rivalry in Europe was too bitter and too near home. Two Balkan wars were damped down. But the third in 1914, beginning with the local murder of a ducal pair, moved up the scale of escalation until virtually the entire human race was involved.

Nor did the peace of 1919 bring a lasting settlement. The successor states of Eastern Europe and the Balkans were too weak, too precarious, and too hostile to each other to provide a sound alternative based on self-determination. A new imperialism rose in Nazi Germany with the old ambition—to seize the successor states of the Turkish empire and defeat all Russian pretensions to the same area. It took a coalition of the whole world to defeat that purpose.

Today it is not difficult to identify on a worldwide scale the "mush areas" and also the rising centers of power. The disputed lands lie in Southeast Asia, in the Middle East, in Africa, and in Latin America where old controls and influences are weakening or have gone. The challengers are old empires with new ideological faces—Russia, China. The defendants are in some measure the outgoing European imperialists, but they are not very active, precisely because they no longer think the imperial game either reputable or worth while. It takes a Sukarno to drag the British unwillingly into Malaysia. The French, after their costly mistakes in Asia, rely on grants and aid, not arms, to keep some kind of a sphere of influence in Africa. This leaves the United States in the odd position of being the only effective counter-power.

America's instinct is undoubtedly to keep clear of the whole post-colonial affair. Its traditions are anticolonial and isolationist. It has no ambition whatsoever to intervene in Africa or Asia. Its desire in Latin America is primarily the old Monroe desire—to keep every non-American Great Power out. But if other Great Powers seek to extend their influence, what then? What is the greater interest—nonintervention or the defense of small nations' rights?

The whole point about "mush areas" is that they positively *invite* outside intervention. This is what their weakness and their internal rivalries lead to. If you have a frontier dispute or a political quarrel with your neighbor and the Chinese happen to be looking over the fence, it is enormously tempting to say: "Look here, Comrade, give me a hand." Then the neighbor yells to Washington: "Look, I'm being pushed out by the Reds." And before the year is out, intervention and escalation may be under way.

This is the old historical fatality. This is how the feuding princes of India in the eighteenth century got the French out. But, inadvertently, they let the British in. In disputed lands, from the dawn of history, local weakness invites local violence; then local defense looks for outside support and, before the world has time to turn round, escalation of the Viet Nam kind is on the way. Southeast Asia, lying between the Great Power spheres of India and China, has been, *par excellence,* such a region of violence and counter-violence for centuries.

One answer to this internal weakness and division is, of course, to accept, permanently, the control of an outside imperial power. Southern China was not always controlled by the "sons of Han" and, for a thousand years, Annam was part of the Chinese empire. But, in the age of self-determination, this solution is presumably ruled out. Are we then condemned, from the sheer incapacity of small communities to protect their own security, to threats of escalation, constantly renewed?

In theory, of course, there are solutions and they are much discussed in the postwar world. One is the regional association in the "mush areas" to bring the small states together into a pattern of power which outside giants will respect and which puts a stop to internal quarreling. The worker in the automobile factory is not content to underline his theoretical equality with the head of General Motors. He joins a union which evens up his effective status and bargaining power. Similarly, smaller nations in wider groupings acquire more of the true characteristics of self-determination.

There is no shortage of regional projects today. Central America is embarked on a remarkably successful economic union. Latin America discusses its proposed free trade area and tries, within the Organization of American States, to build a concensus with its sometimes alarmingly powerful neighbor to the north. The Arabs have, at least theoretically, their Arab League. The Africans struggle to give meaning to the new Organization of African Unity. Even the warring Far East has produced the mythical idea of "Maphilindo"—a union of Malaya, the Philippines, and Indonesia—and most liberal hopes for peace in Viet Nam include the notion of a confederal Southeast Asia held together by the common interest of exploiting the riches of the great Mekong River.

This concept of internal consolidation is one possibility. Clearly it would greatly reinforce the ideas of "positive neutrality" and "nonalignment" very sensibly supported by some leaders in the developing world—I say, sensibly because the very best thing for the peace of the world is that small nations should resist the temptation to take sides in outside quarrels and engulf themselves in Great Power disputes. But, of course, they cannot do so and at the same time try to bring in the Great Powers to arbitrate their own local quarrels. It is only when they give up the fun and excitement of local disputes that creative "nonalignment" becomes a real possibility.

But regional groupings are not the whole answer. Internal disputes may persist and even the most consolidated region can still have a quarrel with an outside power. What then?

Once again, we have a theoretical answer which, timidly, we even occasionally put into practice. This is the concept of an impartial, international police force which can put a stop to violence and keep some kind of truce while peaceful means of solving the problem are explored. The system has all the marks of an infant's first uncertain steps. Trouble arises, say, in

Cyprus. We get soldiers in. We do not have any ready. We have no money, and, anyway, some Powers have not yet paid for the last exercise. Every six months we have a crisis. It is a ludicrous method of running vital human affairs, but nonetheless, the experiment has started—the first genuinely post-national experiment yet made in the critical field of security and peaceful settlement.

The "blue berets" of the U.N. have kept peace in the Gaza strip for over a decade. They held India and Pakistan in a sort of truce over Kashmir for as long. In the Congo, the biggest effort yet made at least prevented a Viet Nam situation from developing there. To buy time and keep the big fellows out may well be, in some crises, the most vital contribution that can be made to peace and if, when trouble erupts, our first instinct is to reach for the United Nations, we may find we have made the first halting step away from the dreadful heights that overlook Armageddon.

Given the provisional and preliminary character of the whole experiment, it may not be fatal that, as a result of Soviet and French objections above all to the Congo operation, peacekeeping through the U.N. seems likely, for some time to come, to be on a voluntary basis, as in Cyprus. Great Power agreement, through the Security Council, would be very difficult to achieve, given the continuance of the Cold War atmosphere; yet speedy action by an international force at the outbreak of trouble remains the best method of checking escalation. Voluntary action through the U.N. Assembly may entail only partial financing. Equally, it is much less easily vetoed.

The interposition of a peace force is, in a sense, a minimal function. It does no more than check the sickening plunge to war. But, conceivably, it could be extended to cover agreed methods of settling the conflict itself. For instance, in Santo Domingo, the aim of the OAS force put together by the United States and the Organization of American States is to remain until impartial elections have produced a government acceptable to the people. In the fifties, the Saar's fate was decided by a supervised plebiscite. One of the weaknesses in India's posture over Kashmir has been its refusal to keep its earlier promise of supervised consultation. There are thus some small signs of the international community feeling its way towards procedures in which, when violence erupts, an international force takes over, creates conditions of reasonable order, keeps out external intervention, and then supervises the submission of a solution—a new government, a new status, a new territorial arrangement —to a popular referendum. Such a solution might be the ultimate way out of the impasse in Viet Nam, both sides accepting popular consultation on government, reunion, neutralization, and guarantees against outside intervention. Admittedly, we still seem light-miles away from such an outcome, but possibly an essential preliminary has to be the realization that there can be no outright victory in Southeast Asia and compromise is infinitely less costly than violent stalemate.

As for the more general reaction that not only a solution in Viet Nam but any elaboration of the international police function properly belongs to Cloud Cuckoo Land, one can perhaps point out that one of the first legal, peace-keeping systems in the world—in medieval Britain—began thus partially and locally, the king granting protection to his subjects against the pretensions of his turbulent barons only along certain routes and in certain areas of sanctuary. Perhaps the little U.N. force, holding crisis at bay, is the first small sign of a "king's peace" coming into being in our international society and destined, hopefully, to spread.

However, all moves towards a more even balance of power in the world are hampered at every turn by hard unpalatable facts of economic and political division. For every move towards regional unity, there are two or three shipwrecks on the reefs of sovereignty and interest. The British West Indian Federation failed. Apart from Nigeria, every federal experiment in Africa has failed or threatens to break up (the OAU itself seems to tremble on the edge of foundering). Chinese and Malays find they cannot live together in Malaysia. Nor can Arabs in a United Arab Republic. When it comes to the test, leaders cannot bear to give up the illusion of absolute sovereignty. Frontiers cannot be agreed. Economic unity promises to give too much advantage to the most wealthy and progessive partner and the partner in turn dislikes the idea of subsidizing poor neighbors. It took the violent intervention of the U.N. to keep the wealth of Katanga inside the Congo. Gabon, Ivory Coast, Mauretania, all managed to disentangle themselves from a previous federal framework.

And, quite apart from built-in internal difficulties of sovereignty and economic interest, it is also true that in the last couple of years, some of the élan has gone out of the move towards "post-national" regional groupings. In all human affairs, there is much of fashion and prestige, of belonging to the avant garde of creative experiment. In the aftermath of the horrors of the last war, the "new wave" did not lie with nationalism. The Nazi movement could be seen for what it was, the last sick stage of nationalism's fatal fever. This caricature of

patriotism, devotion, *pietas,* and decent love of country helped
to turn people's minds to a wider ideal in which the existence
of a state boundary did not give men license to maim, burn,
murder, and massacre the human beings on the further side. A
revulsion against stifling tribalism, a renunciation of the sweet
but destructive pleasures of national self-aggrandisement swept
over Europe where nationalist war had reached its ultimate
self-defeat. The continent turned its face to wider loyalties.
The experiment of "making Europe" began.

Aided by the Marshall Plan and by America's creative insistence on joint action, guided by the practical genius of that
incomparable Frenchman, Jean Monnet, the work of European
unity set the world a fashion of tremendous potency. Its astonishing economic success—with standards of living and rates of
growth surpassing anything achieved in Europe before—its
moving political triumph in reconciling France and Germany,
the old tribal adversaries, its social achievements such as ending Italy's desperate burden of hopeless unemployment—all
these "miracles" helped to convince leaders in other lands,
looking for ways out of their own obstructions, that the nation-
state was not enough. Regional elbowroom had to be added.
The world's keen, rising, and creative interest in regional consolidation had much of its roots in the European experiment.
By the same token, nationalist pretensions have grown and the
élan of cooperation and association has been discouraged
round the world by the sharp loss of momentum in Europe
since 1963.

This slowdown represents a tragic loss of initiative. Europe
is, after all, in some senses, the largest "mush area" in the

world. In spite of the vigor, the variety, the self-consciousness, and sophistication of the national communities which compose it, they are outclassed in power by the Russian and American titans beyond their borders. And in the immediate aftermath of the war a typically "Balkan" situation existed in Europe. In some measure, it was a genuine inheritance from the old Balkan crisis. The "Eastern Question," descended from the collapse of Turkey, still proved to be debatable. Nazi Germany had tried the traditional solution of conquest and annexation to the East. Now the Soviets, as heirs to the czars, undertook counter-occupation, in part to end the uncertainty on their own frontiers, in part to extend their own power, in part—substituting Communism for the old pan-Slavism—to exercise ideological control.

Since Western Europe was still shattered by war and Communism has in any case a universalist appeal, the chance that Russia's intervention might spread still further westward drew in America as guarantor of Western Europe and, up to a point, as guardian of a rival ideology. Thus Europe emerged from the war in two camps, divided by faith and fear and a prey to all the instabilities of any area uneasily split between rival patriots and rival beliefs. The two rivals cannot, it is true, be equated. Russia's intervention was by force, America's by invitation. But instability in Europe has persisted as the inevitable consequence.

There is, of course, no possibility of the present pattern becoming stable. No natural political watershed has been established, with political lines running spontaneously East and West. The line of division even bisects Europe's most powerful national community, and there is no reason to suppose a nation as self-conscious and articulate as the German nation will accept a division imposed on no other advanced state. In fact, the postwar pattern has started to disintegrate. Revived nationalism in Eastern Europe frets away Russian control. General de Gaulle seeks to exclude American influence from Western Europe and—possibly—substitute his own.

Yet the "solution" which these changes presage is no solution either. To rebuild Europe on the old exclusive sovereignties makes little sense economically. The units are too small and require a wider supranational framework and trans-Atlantic cooperation to avoid the disasters of the 1929 depression. It makes even less sense politically. The revival of sovereign nationalism in Europe leads directly to the revival of German nationalism and, with it, the drive to restore unity to the largest, most industrious, most skillful and least trusted people of the continent. Given the memories of 1914 and 1939, neither Russia nor Eastern Europe can accept such an outcome. But if they do not, neither will a revived Germany accept the inferior status of division. There is the stuff here of deadlock and violence. If wars could come as a result of a divided Korea or a divided Viet Nam, it is fatuous optimism to assume no such risk in a still divided Germany. Moreover, conflict in Europe could not be contained. This is where war, from the start, would threaten to be total.

Yet in theory at least we need not dismiss the European dilemma as insoluble. The solution is, in fact, a version of the pattern proposed for other "mush areas"—internal consolidation, external guarantees. If the German nation is solidly embedded in a web of supranational interests, interdependences, institutions, and authorities which enlarge its economic and social potential while restricting its political sovereignty, then German reunion is no longer a danger. Nor will restricted sovereignty be resented by Germany if the restrictions are shared by all its neighbors.

The first strong trend towards such an outcome came to life as a result of the Marshall Plan and the movement towards European unity. Up to 1963, one could envisage a steady widening of the initiative. The Common Market of the Six was the nucleus of effective supranational institutions. Then, it could be hoped, Britain and the Scandinavians would join, greatly strengthening the liberal outward-looking nature of the association. Its vast attractive power in terms of economic dynamism —which had already overcome Britain's old-fashioned insularity—was beginning to make its appeal to the Eastern Europeans increasingly dissatisfied with satellite status and never very enchanted by the ideological issue. One could envisage a steady "opening to the East" in the enlarged Common Market offering possibly, in time, associate-membership to the Easterners and some form of confederal arrangement linking West and East Germany.

Such changes would not weaken either American or Russian economic interests in the area. On the contrary, the more prosperous and dynamic the continent, the more its neighbors would need to concert economic policy with it—on trade, on liquidity, on international investment, on all the issues raised by the need to maintain a functioning *world* economy. But the changes would, step by step, change the strategic outlook. If a hostile line of defense no longer lay through the heart of Europe, one could envisage not "disengagement"—with its suggestion that in the age of the intercontinental missile America can, in any meaningful sense, "withdraw" across an ocean its weapons can cross in a few minutes—but rather a joint "engagement" of both neighbors to guarantee and respect the integrity of the area. True, such an outcome presupposed genuine *détente* between the United States and the Soviet Union, but such an attitude began to appear on both sides as the 1960s advanced.

But these more hopeful possibilities for the dangerous European "mush area" have been weakened by General de Gaulle's activities since 1963. It is true that one of the excuses he puts forward for his confused and confusing policies is that only if he can remove American influence from Europe will Russia accept German reunification as part of the unity of Europe "from the Atlantic to the Urals"—whatever that may mean. But, in fact, the General's premises are false. By breaking the momentum of the Common Market's extension to include Britain, he began to jeopardize the existing institutions of unity. Confidence and élan are part of the living tissue of any political experiment and he damaged both with his veto on a British entry that was earnestly supported by the other five. Nor has his subsequent insistence on imposing French minority views done anything but increase the Community's weakness.

At the same time, while the growing point of genuinely supranational institutions—into which a reunited Germany can finally be incorporated—continues to wilt, the total national sovereignty the General claims for France—including the appalling prestige symbol of one's own personal atom bomb—raises the old demons elsewhere. The language of unrestrained sovereignty is heard again in Germany. Even if the djinn is not yet out of the bottle, General de Gaulle's constant rubbing—and rubbing in—of the old exclusive claims to total nationhood feeds the old egoisms and the old passions.

Above all, his pathological reaction to American influence in Europe jeopardizes the whole possibility of any peaceful reunification of Europe. Ultimately no one doubts—least of all the Americans—that the European continent will be nobody's satellite. The problem is how to get from the present fading but still effective division to the later unity. Here America's part is indispensable.

The chief obstacle to union has already been described— Russia's attitude to German reunification. Reunification in peace can only be with Russia's consent and any attempt at reunification without peace means atomic annihilation. Russia is not likely to be persuaded along the path towards consent unless two opposite moods can be induced at once—restraint and reassurance. Restraint is needed to discourage the Stalinist wing in Russia from believing that changes in Germany's status will give new opportunities for Communist intervention in West Germany. Reassurance is needed to encourage the Russians to believe that a reunited Germany is no added threat to their security.

Equally, the same balance of moods is needed in Germany —restraint to discourage any Cold War warriors from seeking unity by violence and seeing it as a basis for yet another wave of conquest in the Ukraine, reassurance to guarantee that peaceful diplomacy will in fact bring reunification about. Clearly, to achieve this balance of firmness and persuasion, this cross between discouragement and friendship, requires diplomacy of the utmost delicacy and strength. Only the United States has the power, prestige, and detachment needed to carry it through.

France lacks the sheer power either to restrain a revived nationalism in Germany or to offer Germany any guarantees of reunion in peace. Equally, the French nation is too negligible militarily to make any impact on Russia except in so far as French anti-Americanism suggests a weakness worth probing in the West. As such, it encourages any remaining adventurism in Russia and weakens the arguments for the peaceful acceptance of reunification.

Only the United States is strong enough both to restrain nationalism in Germany and to offer the hope of eventual reunification. Only America is strong enough to reassure Russia that reunification offers no military threat but that probing in the West is dangerous and fruitless. Few nations have had to face so delicate a diplomatic assignment and it is here, above all, that effective policy requires a "sense of direction" which leads beyond the immediate upheavals and disappointments and tends steadily towards a future secure Europe based on internal unity and external guarantees.

Indeed, what other direction can one envisage? The mood in Britain for joining the continent has sharply improved. There is more interest in Europe—and especially in Germany—in widening the opportunities of the community eastwards just as the Eastern countries begin to look westward for wider trade. America continues its efforts to maintain the *détente* with Russia. In these conditions, there exists at least the possibility of reviving the ideal of a Europe ultimately united and enjoying close external relations with *two* large and friendly neighbors.

Meanwhile the task is to live out General de Gaulle's period of office and pick up again the tasks of unity once his remarkable but anachronistic figure has taken its place in the historical record to which he already in spirit belongs.

If the search for unity becomes once again Europe's paramount business, this development alone will help to blow new life into experiments of regional association elsewhere. No doubt, one cannot expect quick results. From Joan of Arc to Louis XIV, from Henry V to the "Glorious Revolution" of 1688, it took nearly four centuries to evolve the tough, ruthless, and enormously effective institution of the nation-state. However anachronistic this political form may be in the age of the atom bomb, the world economy, and the super-states, it will not be easily transcended, either by those who have enjoyed its supposedly untrammeled sovereignty for some time or by those who, in the wake of de-colonization, think they have just secured it.

Yet one may hope that mankind will be able to shorten the period of gestation for new associations which are more capable of providing their citizens with economic welfare and more able to provide security against the possible pressures of vast neighbors. Nobody, after all, planned the nation-state. It sprang in part from the chances of history and geography but in part from the logic of growing worldwide economic rivalry and from insistent demands for more popular participation in the government. Today, geography and history will still determine where regional associations are most likely to develop. Argentina will not federate with Nigeria. But the logic of events—of economic interdependence, of "rising expectations," of the neighborhood of vast super-powers, of atomic risks—all point beyond the small community. The nationalist, in this age

of a world society, may well be as obsolete as the dynast on the
verge of the age of democracy. This does not mean he will van-
ish painlessly. The dynasts too fought and still fight rearguard
actions. The hope is that he will be eclipsed before his obsolescence leads to ultimate disaster.

Yet even if we suppose that good sense and the logic of history encourage men to end the fatal weakness of Balkanized
"mush areas" which invite external intervention, we are still
left with the giants. Is a gradual extension of the "king's peace"
enough if the recalcitrant barons remain as powerful and unruly as ever? The world may be held, for the time being, in a
sort of security based on a balance of terror. But it is an appall-
ingly precarious base. Do we face no better foundation for
world order than the Great Powers' possibly mutual but certainly unpoliced disinclination to blow each other up?

True, such restraint does in itself represent some progress.
This is the first time in man's record that war has worn so uncompromisingly a destructive face that no one weighing the
risks of war can have the illusion of emerging as a victor. This
is why direct attacks, Great Power on Great Power, are unlikely. This is why it is even conceivable that if Small Powers,
like Britain or France, or—for the time being (in terms of actual military strength)—China, were to threaten their neighbors with their mini-atomic capability, the two super-powers,
Russia and America, might cooperate to discourage them. In
fact, probably the only real danger in the possible proliferation of atomic weapons could lie in an angry, aroused, nationalist Germany coming to control its own bomb. Even then the
danger would spring more from Russian fears than German
capabilities.

Yet France's decision to have its own prestige bomb as the mark of Great Powerhood can lead directly to a German demand for the same kind of status—unless German security and German *amour propre* are secured by other means. In the long run, a united Europe, guaranteed by both its neighbors, may have its own bomb, with a very reassuring number of fingers on the trigger. Or it may, together with its neighbors, sensibly decide to give up these bogeyman terrors. But we still have to get from our present divided condition to that hoped-for unity.

The whole point behind any Atlantic nuclear arrangement is, obviously, to mesh German defense so closely in with America's that the Germans feel both secure and interdependent. This crucial factor is not yet clear to the Russians. They persist in arguing that if any such arrangement includes Germany, it is a step toward further atomic proliferation. In fact it is the opposite since the alternative—given the trend to purely national nuclear armament set by France—could be, sooner or later, such a genuine act of proliferation as the appearance of the all-German bomb. Compared with this risk, multilateral arrangements are security itself. However, it is possible that they need not be pushed to anything as elaborate as the old multilateral force which the Russians have fixedly opposed. They could, for insance, mean simply close formal consultation on nuclear strategy combined with nuclear training.

Yet the compromise, whatever it may be, will still depend upon the balance of mutual terror. Is this then all we can hope for? Have we to rely on stalemate between the great barons? It seems a precarious enough peace. But there are some reassuring factors. The greatest barons of all—the United States and the Soviet Union—have in fact reached a number of points of implicit agreement. Since the Cuban confrontation, they are fairly clear that atomic weapons cannot be used to alter the existing balance of power. They have formally agreed through the test-ban treaty not to pollute the air breathed by their own citizens and by all mankind. They would like to agree on some control of the further spread of nuclear weapons. This may not be a recipe for total peace. But it is light-miles away from the preliminaries to total war.

Their desire not to alter the existing power balance by violence means caution in all areas where dangerous confrontations are possible. This points to some mitigation of the risks in the "mush areas." These, of course, remain the most likely sources of conflict and of escalation into unplanned but unavoidable general war. If, in addition to Great Power restraint, the techniques of local consolidation and international supervision can be successfully elaborated over the next decades, the worst trouble spots will be brought under some sort of control. Better still, examples of successful peace-keeping will begin to alter and enlarge and diversify the way in which people are ready to think about national security.

The next point is the astonishing and appalling cost of armaments. The developed world spends $140,000 millions a year on security systems which give them no more than the precarious balance of mutual terror. It is possible to wonder whether this price may not come to seem excessive. If, twenty or thirty years from now, regional police forces are providing a framework of security at 1/140,000 of the cost in all the "mush areas," may not the electorates of the Great Powers notice the contrast? They may begin to think of all the benefits for themselves and their children which $140,000 million or so a year might procure; they might suggest to their rulers that what is good for a "mush area" is good for a Great Power too. They might even *ask* whether international police and methods of peaceful settlement could not be usefully extended to the globe itself.

Once this conviction takes the place of panic, concern over a state of "national security" which grows more and more insecure as the arms bill rises, then the organization of a general security system through the United Nations will enter the realm of practical politics. The "king's peace" will begin to become not the exception, but the rule.

How one then organizes "the king's" authority must be left for the future. Majority voting in an enlarged Security Council with some weighting of votes for the larger states—which by then clearly should include China—is one possibility. But such a central authority is unlikely to precede peoples' readiness for it. The urgent task now is to create on a local basis the working models of international police and peace and then trust to humanity's common sense to think the experiment worth extending to all mankind.

And the possibility of such a shift in world opinion is linked in turn with another. May not the scientific and technological revolutions of our day produce a yet unguessed mutation in human attitudes? We have lived through the millennia on the basis of shortage. How will mankind react if relative plenty becomes the norm? In the past, conquest and imperialism, war and violence have had their roots deep in the fact of absolute shortage. The desire to take your neighbor's land, to lay hold of his resources, to overcome your inadequacies by making his life more inadequate still—have not these been, again and again, the bitter causes of aggression? And in so far as nations recognize the dearth and feel beset by the need for "living space," they almost instinctively choose for leaders men who articulate these violent needs and envies. Prosperous people very rarely choose lunatics for rulers. But Germany, with nine million men out of work and hunger in the streets, chose Hitler.

Is it then too audacious to hope that if, in the next decades, most of mankind can be set, by way of the new technologies, on the path of growth, then human conquest—which used to be for slaves and land and treasure—may now become the conquest of things of the mind, of the inventions which flow from science, of the "inner space" of human imagination and capacity? Nor need we exclude the high adventure of "outer space." Just possibly, the age of bloody physical conquest which has lasted for a hundred thousand years—from the tribe to the empire—may now be reaching its term. If the triumphs and contests of abundance take the place of the old grinding enmities bred of scarcity, then, perhaps, we shall not destroy ourselves. We shall not find it entirely irrational to live in hope.

THREE

The Balance of Wealth

The end of ancient shortage may mean a more peaceful world. Equally, we are not within sight of either yet. On the contrary, the present disproportions of wealth in the world community are themselves a cause of conflict. If everybody is poor, you may get the acquiescent peace of a tribal village. If everyone has enough, there is some chance of a more dynamic kind of content. But today the world suffers from contrasts between riches and poverty—internationally, regionally, and locally—which seem enough to incite the sufferers to the most violent protest.

We are becoming familiar with the facts about these contrasts. Indeed, we are in some danger of making truisms of them before we have fully realized them to be true. In the "North" of our planet—above the Tropic of Cancer—about a quarter of the human race enjoys some 75 percent of its trade, investment, and resources. The minority is largely white and European in origin and lives in market economies. But the exceptions show that this concentration is probably temporary. Russia is only three-quarters white and three-quarters European and, before long, may only be three-quarters planned. Japan belongs to the club only as a market economy—in spite of being counted an "honorary European" in South Africa, a community which, in common with some other stratified societies, often permits wealth to determine acceptability. And perhaps wealth *is* the chief hallmark of this northern "club" which includes white and colored, European and Asian, planned and free.

But there are regional disparities which are almost as troublesome. The Mediterranean fringes of Europe have not yet joined fully in its prosperity, in spite of the golden growing flood of tourists. Soviet Asia's mineral wealth has not yet offset its appalling climate and lack of migrants. All through the developing world, economies with exploitable resources—above all minerals—lie next door to mountains and deserts where wretched farmers and pastoralists scratch a living. And since in any modernized economy, some scale of market is a precondition of growth, these marginal communities are in the trap of small numbers providing few outlets, few outlets discouraging higher production, and inadequate production keeping the numbers low. Their one hope is in regional economic arrangements but these, as we have seen, smack too much of sharing to be swallowed easily by wealthier neighbors. Then, at the domestic level, profound disparities persist between social groups and classes. In short, if there is a long scale of power in the world from the super-powers down to the micro-states, so, too, there is a ladder of wealth which in many ways coincides with the scale of wealth, above all, at the top where no state can carry a full nuclear armament without vast resources and skills mobilized to meet the cost. And the instability inherent in unbalanced power is repeated and reinforced by unbalanced wealth. The poor states are under pressure from the hopes and expectations of their own people. If pressure turns to revolt, the temptation to ask for outside help is only equalled, in these ideological days, by the temptation to give it. Either way, we are back with the risks of escalation and nuclear war.

At present, the gaps are actually tending to widen. The countries at the bottom of the scale are about holding their present levels of poverty. They grow by about 2 to 3 percent a year. But so do their birthrates. About half way up the ladder a few countries—in the $200 to $300 per capita income range —are bounding ahead. Mexico, Greece, Israel, Taiwan have been growing by over 6 percent a year in terms of per capita gross national product—the sum of all the community's goods and services. Then, in the upper reaches, countries which are rich already have been adding 3 to 4 percent a year to their per capita GNP. With stable populations, steady employment, and rising productivity they have encountered few obstacles to sustained growth. This steady surge has, in the case of the United States, brought the gross national product up to some $630,000 millions in 1964 and allowed, in the same year, an increase of over $30,000 millions. Thus, in a single year, America *added* to its GNP the equivalent of the whole of Africa's current wealth or 50 percent of Latin America's—both continents with a higher population. Such in our day are the gigantic differences in resources between the high and the low on the scale of wealth.

What has happened in the last two centuries to create this singular lopsidedness? The short answer is that the wealthy areas are those in which the modern technological revolution has taken place. The differences are not of absolute wealth for, in a world of accelerating invention, wealth itself is an uncertain concept. Yesterday's valueless pitchblende is tomorrow's priceless uranium. Today's gold could be tomorrow's teeth fillings if the international economy were genuinely to move away from an old-fashioned bullion base. Denmark has turned its sandy soils into wealth by the scientific development of bacon. The fertile slopes of the eastern Andes are hardly farmed at all for lack of people and capital. No pre-scientific prophet would ever have picked two small islands with relatively meager resources—Britain and Japan—as pioneers of the new technological society in the West and then in the East. They could not have foreseen that wealth would now consist not so much in physical endowment as in skill, invention, discovery, in the instruments of the new technology, and in the capacity to accumulate enough capital to invest in them. This is the essence of the revolution of abundance, and it may sound simple. But it is not. To bring the two aspects of modernization—technology and saving—together successfully means an almost complete reordering of society—in short, a revolution and not least in the minds of men.

Moreover, it is a continuous revolution. So far, at least, there is no stage in the process at which a society can congratulate itself on having found a stable answer. The process of "taking off" into sustained growth—into the ability to save, invest, and go on saving—is only the first problem. Staying in the air and climbing higher can be just as difficult, especially since, as the flight goes on, one can meet economic ice storms, alto cumulus of new competitive inventions, side winds from neglected agriculture, and, from time to time, passengers who have smuggled dynamite on board. As men have discovered, often painfully in the economies of the West, the journey can be as arduous as the start and economies encounter different hazards according to the point in time of their take-off. The adventure of economic modernizaton and growth is perhaps more like an obstacle race than a "breakthrough." The first hazard, from sheer inexperience, may seem the highest, but, in fact, societies reach other thresholds of difficulty later on which may demand quite as much ingenuity to negotiate. The British, for instance, were the inventors of the new economy. Today, indebted, over-importing, under-exporting, insufficiently competitive, and apparently apathetic, they seem to have traveled far from Victorian optimism, let alone Elizabethan drive. Or, starting from a different point of departure and a different set of premises, the Russian economy today finds that not even the most vigorous central planning can bring comfortably together Soviet Asia where power and minerals are in surplus and Soviet Europe where people and machines cry out for resources. Sometimes the blight is general. In what sort of shape did any member of the Western industrial community look in 1931? It is just as important to study the various obstacles to growth along the route as to have a clear picture of how the whole process started.

The origins in Britain made clear the decisive importance of technological discovery and invention on the one hand and savings on the other. It was in Britain that, first in any community, the best minds gave themselves to "natural philosophy" —or the study of material things. In part this was a conscious revulsion from the fanatical theologies of the recent Wars of

Religion which had played some part in Britain's own Civil War. The Royal Society was established by temperate philosophers like John Locke and undogmatizing clerics like Bishop Stubbs precisely to discover a universe of discourse which could be relied on not to divide intelligent men. The eighteenth century became *par excellence* the experimenting century when citizens from dukes to artisans conducted, virtually in their own back gardens, passionate enquiries into the behavior of practically everything—minerals, metals, machines, plants, steam power, water power. Out of this interest and work a stream of "improvements" began to flow.

And it met the counter-stream of savings. Pre-Reformation Europe had developed a banking system, above all for foreign trade. But the Puritans enormously strengthened it since they had unconsciously discovered the supreme recipe for capital accumulation—work with religious zeal since the resulting fortune is a sign of God's blessing, but spend none of it for luxury is a sign of Popish decadence. Then the maritime people of Western Europe, more and more conscious of their separate nationhood, began to compete all round the world to bring home the spoils of trade from the rich Orient. Bankers and merchants throve still more. The banking system spread through the country and began to draw in savings from wider groups. The development of the joint stock company enabled even small investors to join in. In eighteenth-century Britain, fortunes were also growing as worldwide British commercial predominance increased, particularly in India with the collapse of Mughal power. The returning merchant-plunderers from Bengal were named "moguls" as they repatriated vast sums and set themselves up in the cool, lovely, Palladian country

houses which adorn the novels of Jane Austen and Thackeray.
Warren Hastings was perhaps "amazed at his own moderation." Others were not and their fortunes swelled the flow of
capital.

Inventions, capital, effective economic institutions—in every
"breakthrough" these have proved to be essential preconditions
of success. But they require a fourth—the entrepreneur who
gets the "mix" of all the elements right and acts so that his activities are genuinely productive, in other words, produce
more for less—less work, less time, less resources, less money.
The "more for less" is the essential secret of the whole process,
for only in this way does the surplus emerge for further investment, further productivity, and a still larger surplus. The entrepreneur may be of any type—the banker, the artisan, the
businessman, the duke, the commissar. But without him, the
world would have nothing but a trail of private bankruptcies
or public enterprises working at a loss. He is the rarest element
in any economy—the reason the successful manager in public
or private economies commands the highest rewards.

In the first British experiment, the entrepreneur was the private innovator. He it was who first combined a passionate interest in the uses of the new technology with the shrewd realization that, with capital applied to it, it would produce more
for less and leave him with a profit. Two hungers of man met
—curiosity and cupidity. They have proved a formidable
combination.

John Wilkinson, for instance, had a single passion—the uses
of iron ore. He spent his life experimenting with new methods
of ironworking and along the way he became a modern capitalist with an integrated business from iron mines in Cornwall

to iron foundries in Le Creusot. He made everything in iron. He even made a church in iron, heaven help us. To indulge his passion, he invested his own money, his wife's money, all his friends' money, any money he could lay his hands on, in all possible means of expanding the iron industry. This was the first, the essential combination. He brought science and technology, savings and entrepreneurial risk together in the fruitful relationship which is still the basis of our technological revolution.

But he was only one of a thousand busy men, and they were active in every sector of the economy. There is Coke of Holkham who, by inventing a new rotation of crops and by marling his fields, quadrupled the output of agriculture. Or there is the Duke of Bridgewater, appropriately named since water—bridging it, ditching it, draining it, canalizing it—was his life. He helped drain the rich corn land of the Fens and built the canals which halved the cost of transport from Britain's industrial north to the markets in the south. No phrase was more ill-chosen to describe the technological breakthrough in Britain than "the industrial revolution." It was a *general* revolution in productivity—more productive farming, more productive transport, new industry, more sophisticated methods of accounting and financing—everywhere the "more for less" which flows from applying trained intelligence to human resources. To suggest an industrial predominance has misled generations of developers since. Would Stalin have neglected agriculture so catastrophically if he had realized that more productive farms are an essential factor in modernization? It was part of the extraordinary insight of the Japanese that when, a century after the British, they began the acceleration of innovation and investment essential to a "breakthrough," they made a root and branch land reform and a very considerable investment in agriculture a central feature of their economic revolution.

To return to the British origins of the system, one might expect, in such conditions of revolution and expansion, to find a sense of excitement and achievement among the men who studied the phenomenon—the new class of economists as they came to be called. Certainly, there is a sense of exhilaration and optimism in Adam Smith. He felt that the new methods did promise a breakthrough to new and better ways of ordering society. The whole of mankind would benefit from an international division of labor based upon developing countries, each producing what it was best fitted to produce and breaking away from narrow mercantilist restrictions and efforts at self-sufficiency which, Smith thought, made not much more sense at the national than at the village level. His ideal of a "great commercial republic" was an ideal of liberation, of growth, of expansion, and also of neighborliness and peace.

But by the end of the Napoleonic Wars and the onslaught of the first postwar depression, the mood was less cheerful. In fact, in was downright discouraged and not for nothing did economics earn the title of the "dismal science." Without much exaggeration, one can say that some of the most notable early economists hardly believed that the new economic system could survive. We have, of course, to remember that the new economy was completely unfamiliar and no one could say for certain what it was that made it work. It is very easy to assume that something is pretty precarious if you do not know how to

turn on the engine. But the fears were more explicit than a
general ignorance. One of them we have already mentioned—
the discovery of "the margin." If on the one hand, resources
and skills are limited, and on the other, people tend to pay less
for a thing the more they have of it, there is obviously a point
at which the "more for less" will not work. As materials and
skilled labor become more sought for and used up, they grow
more expensive. But at the same time purchasers whose first
eagerness has been satisfied will tend to pay less—hence, rising
costs, falling earnings, smaller profits, and finally no profits. At
this point, growth stops because it is not worth anyone's while
to go on investing and producing. And so long as society relies
on private investors for virtually all its economic decisions,
then an end of profits must mean the slowing down or stop-
page of the whole economy.

Ricardo had a particular and concrete fear. He saw the
processes of farming in England gradually absorbing the rich
river bottoms; then they would creep over the less cultivata-
ble downs. At last, reaching the Welsh and Pennine ranges,
they would encounter the limits of profitable development.
Thereafter only very high food prices would allow for further
expansion. But these, entailing higher wages all round, would
cripple profits everywhere else. The system, precariously balanced on the razor's edge of profitability, would break down.
Ricardo could not, of course, foresee how quickly the New
World's massive grain production—on the prairies of North
and South America—would be drawn in, via the repeal of the
tariffs on corn, to redress the balance in old England. This
change was a vindication of Adam Smith's robust confidence
and an early sign that the new economy, considered on a

global scale, contained the promise of almost limitless productivity. But these changes lay in the future. Meanwhile, there were other worries.

A further source of pessimism—and one, I think, that strikes a chord today—was the belief that the working class, in their incontinence, would go on breeding children up to the limit imposed by sheer survival. Any increase in wages would be followed not by any increase in savings, thrift, or respectability, but simple by more progeny, more young, more "proles"— from which propensity, incidentally, is derived the term "proletarian." This nineteenth-century feeling about the breeding habits of the poor class has much in common with the twentieth-century feeling about birthrates in the poor nations. In the wake of Malthus, hundreds of worthy men and women felt a certain helplessness when faced with the teeming slums. What could be done about such irresponsibility? It was not simply a social problem. The whole future of the economy was involved. If the mass of potential consumers could never, owing to their breeding habits, raise themselves above mere subsistence, how could they produce either the savings needed for expansion or a buoyant enough market to absorb all the goods the new machines were beginning to pour out?

And to round out the picture of Victorian pessimism, we must add the potent figure of Karl Marx. He was in one sense no pessimist. Alone among the early analysts, he realized and welcomed the colossal revolution of resources introduced by the new entrepreneurs. He saw that they were remaking the face of the earth, opening the way to possibilities of unparalleled abundance, and that society would never be the same again as a result of their activities. But he was a pessimist in the short run for he believed both in Ricardo's margin and in Malthus' proletarians—but he gave a much more radical explanation for the phenomena. All wealth, he claimed, had its source in labor. But if the laboring classes were deprived of the full fruits of their effort by an exploiting class of capitalists owning the means of production and squeezing out all the profits for themselves, then, naturally, the internal market would not grow to keep pace with the productivity of the new machines. Demand was bound to be inadequate to absorb the new supply since the distribution of effective purchasing power to the consuming many was blocked by the accumulation of wealth by the owning few.

We will turn in a moment to the reasons why Marx and all his contemporaries were wrong about the resilience and success of the market economy. But before we do so, two points should be made about Marx's contribution. He did foresee that the creation of effective demand would be the crucial problem in the development of the market economy. And even if his labor theory of value is now seen to be very dubious economics, he was very far from being a dubious moralist and prophet. His real force wells up from the tremendous sense of responsibility and judgment on the Jewish social tradition. He could not, any more than a Jeremiah or an Ezekiel, tolerate the serious, complacent faces of the bourgeois around him, congratulating themselves on doing God's work while little children fell to their death in the machinery in the cotton mills. In theory, no doubt, there was no place for his moral indignation. As a good Marxist he had to argue that capitalists were only behaving according to the class pattern laid out for them by the iron laws of history. Nor were proletarians any more independent of their fixed destiny. But Marx was a better prophet than theorist. He remained exceedingly, vituperatively, angry and that anger has gone on playing an overwhelming role in modern society long after any very detailed interest in his economic theories had begun to recede.

When we come to the reasons the gloomy prophecies of Marx and most of his contemporaries have failed to take effect, we leave the first breakthrough to the modern economy and follow instead the course of its spreading, headlong, sometimes calamitous, and always unpredictable development round the world. Today, with hindsight, we can see how it is that, so far, as the obstacles to growth have emerged, policies have also appeared to steer the experiment round and over them. If one generalization can be noted to sum up this process, it can be said to consist in the slow, uncertain, unfolding realization that in the modern economy, stability and growth ultimately depend not so much on the organization of supply but on the maintenance of buoyant demand. But this fact did not appear graven on stone. It is a pragmatic discovery. In following the historical record, we can see how often the policies had little to do with the specific difficulty and solved it, as it were, on the side. Only later could cause and effect be put together. This fact should increase both the hopefulness and the modesty of those concerned with economic development. Human society does seem to have some way out of its dilemmas but not necessarily by the route it thought it was taking.

We will look first at developments inside the national economy and try to catch both the extraordinary, undirected diversity and also the ultimate effectiveness of the expedients which the modern economy lurched into and adopted along its uncertain route. One factor has been touched on already—the unexpected productiveness of the new technology and the elbowroom it gave for greater purchasing power. War may have been the forcing house here but invention, curiosity, and experiment, encouraged by the hope of profit, played a vital and continuous part. It is true that while the first great costly installations of the new economy were being put in place, not even rising productivity allowed much surplus purchasing power to be left over for the mass of the people. Whether they were the new workers heading into Manchester and Birmingham, or raw migrants arriving in New York, or the Kazakh nomads pitchforked into the first steel towns of the Urals, all the surplus they helped to create was directed, by capitalists or by commissars, into further capital construction. These, in Marx's phrase, were the tough days of "primitive accumulation" and without them, the rhythm of expansion would not have been established. But they have always been hard. They are so again today in India or China. Once, however, the apparatus is in being, it is usually productive enough to allow both wages and profits to grow and thus to allow the mass consumers a larger share of potential purchasing power. The margin is more distant than Ricardo thought.

Moreover, as the century advanced, it became clear all through Western Europe that workers, faced with the choice of raising and educating a few children well or simply multiplying, took the more responsible course. In fact, after one world war and one world depression, their enthusiasm for progeny had declined to the point of threatening the community's survival. Gloomy demographers plotted the year in which the whole population of Sweden or France would be

over fifty years of age. Malthus had still to be disproved elsewhere. But the Atlantic world began to produce manageable
birthrates. With Ricardo and Malthus both in retreat and the
phase of "primitive accumulations" over, real wages began,
after 1860, to increase, first in Britain, then in Europe and
North America—a process which was not much checked until
the early 1900s.

Then, as the twentieth century developed, the various economies came upon new expedients. The share available for general consumption was once again transformed and increased
by the introduction of mass production methods, primarily in
the United States. The need to find machines simple and
repetitive enough for handling by ignorant immigrant workers
contributed something to the change. Insatiable demand in
war—and the assembly line techniques it called forth—gave
some of the impetus. Managers of genius like Henry Ford
pioneered their general use, raising wages so that the man on
the bench could afford the car he was making. At another
level, it was one more application of Adam Smith's division of
labor. At yet another, it foreshadowed automation and the vir-
tual removal of manual workers from the factory floor. But
short of these later and more apocalyptic consequences, it provided a new range of productivity and with it a new range and
scale of possible consumption.

Another set of expansive policies flowed from the activities
of government. We have already looked at the part played by
war in modifying people's views about the state's acceptable
functions. This modification had to take place because the possible role of government was played down in early theory. It
was rejected by the liberals because they followed Adam

Smith in believing it to be, on the basis of recent experience with mercantilism, inefficient, bumbling, and usually corrupt, and it was dismissed by Marx because he regarded government as simply "the managing committee of the bourgoisie" and believed it would only intervene on the side of the great vested interests.

Up to a point, he was right. Nineteenth-century governments were at first quicker with tariffs and subsidies than with, say, social insurance. But he reckoned without liberal political tradition and independent Christian conscience. Christian reformers in Britain led the struggle to introduce state protection for workers and state intervention against exploitation. "Bourgeois" rights such as the right of association brought workers together in unions and parties. Constitutional precedent gave them the vote. Since they were, inevitably, the majority, their influence was soon felt in benefits voted by parliaments for the mass of the people and an income tax imposed on the rich to finance the benefits—a juster distribution of wealth heartily supported by the reformers. But more than justice was served. As the welfare system grew, its built-in provision of purchasing power in times of unemployment and sickness was discovered to provide yet another safeguard of sustained demand and hence of economic health.

However, these possibilities inherent in government intervention were not realized at first. The theory of public finance had still nothing to do with the use of government power to balance and, when necessary, expand the flow of demand in the economy. On the contrary, the government was supposed to "pay its way" and to keep a balanced budget—in other words, cover its spending by the taxes it brought in. Part of the time this provision simply canceled out government spending. But in times of rapid expansion with revenues rising, the authorities often remitted taxes—since their needs were satisfied —and thus increased the scale of demand pushing the boom upwards. Equally, in bad times, as public revenues fell, government would introduce higher taxes to cover essential expenditure and increase the deflation by withdrawing yet more purchasing power from the shrinking economy. In short, traditional fiscal policy tended to increase the fluctuations of slumps and booms. It was really only after World War II, with its fantastic expansion financed by the arms effort (in other words by government) and its aftermath of a vast unsatisfied civilian purchasing power which could only be brought under control by government, that the auticyclical possibilities of government action began to be realized—increasing demand in slack times, reining it back in times of boom, and at all times seeking full use of expanding resources. The vast collapse of 1929 occurred, after all, in spite of government spending on social insurance and public education and even some public works. The decisive breakthrough came only after World War II with the acceptance by governments of a peace time responsibility to full employment and effective demand. Thus it is an achievement of only the last two decades. In fact, it may well be that, in the United States, the respectability of the need to break away from balanced budgets and accept instead the government's duty of "demand management" was only finally established by the brilliantly successful Kennedy tax cut in 1963.

And, like so many earlier discoveries, the new understanding of the role of demand management may still be precarious. At present, in an economy on the scale of the United States, it can be seen functioning at its peak. With the budget used as a flexible instrument for balancing the flow of demand into the system, with arms and greater welfare sustaining public spending, with sustained mass consumption stimulating an inventive, competitive, private industry, the economy grows by 4 to 5 percent a year, the expectation of future growth stimulates investment in further plant, and growth itself generates more revenue for further welfare. Given these new techniques, it is not impossibly optimistic to believe that the same momentum can be maintained in the coming decade as it has been over the last ten years—and by some of the same methods—within the expanding framework of Europe's Common Market.

But there are at least three reasons for caution. The first is the chance that the technique of "demand management" itself is not yet mastered. The second is that, even if it is, abundance is creating a whole new range of daunting and dangerous possibilities. The third is that the solutions achieved so far apply only to economies operating on a near-continental scale. We shall have to postpone the millennium a little until these three points have been examined.

The chief technical difficulty facing demand management is to prevent the economy from "overheating"—in other words, to prevent demand from running ahead of available supplies. If demand is pushed too hard, then people and institutions begin to try to take more out of the economy than existing supplies can provide. The prices of goods that are becoming scarce go up, the workers who have to buy the more expensive goods bargain for higher wages, and an inflationary spiral can be set moving throughout the economy.

The answer to the risk may seem obvious: to keep the supply of resources—materials, skilled labor, plant capacity, new savings—always a little ahead of demand. In America in the last five years, with abundant food, large stockpiles, a dollar that can buy any material needed abroad, a scale of wealth that generates a flood of savings, and plant working at under 90 percent of capacity, the slack has been there and prices have been stable. But in practice it is not always so easy. Not all economies have such fabulous material resources. Few generate savings on the same scale. Organized workers balk at unemployment and have come to expect regular, almost routine increases in wages. In these conditions, demand—of which wages is the largest component—tends to edge up towards the safety limit and slop over the top, pulling prices up behind it.

There are solutions. Experiments made in Europe since the war have for instance shown that if a government can give its industrialists a longer term picture of sustained and rising demand, they can plan their capital expansion not in disturbing lumps and jerks but on a sustained and hence less inflationary basis. "Indicative planning" of this kind, pioneered by the French, can be formal or informal, but it is a powerful instrument of stable growth.

Some countries—notably Holland—have at times successfully achieved an "incomes policy" whereby the general wage level goes up in step with the economy's increased capacity to produce supplies. Particular industries where labor is scarce may pay more. Declining industries may drop out of the bidding and let their people go. But the workers as a whole get steady increases in real wages, not phoney jumps to new scales which inflation instantly wipes out. The British today are struggling to introduce both techniques into their economy

—indicative planning and an income policy. In America the President's "guide lines" are an unofficial version of a similar tactic. But none can say that these new approaches, possibly essential to successful, noninflationary demand management, have yet fully proved themselves and have therefore come to stay.

The second problem—the question of quality—presupposes success in demand management. It assumes that the new release of resources will last. But it underlines the fact that abundance as such does not solve all problems. In many areas of choice judgment and quality, it only offers the *hope* that the difficulties can be solved. The unplanned drift of the modern economy is producing a number of blights which darken the picture of a successful, let alone a great, society. Urban sprawl, destroying the living natural environment at the fringes and leaving ghettos of squalor at the core, disfigures a technological order which is increasingly urban. The economy's steady demand for higher skills leaves uncared for and despairing the unskilled dropouts of the educational system. In the short run, automation destroys more jobs—precisely in this unskilled category—than it creates. Shortened work weeks to be lived in cities without beauty and space force people back on the most blunting and worthless types of recreation. Add to all these blights the dynamite of racial inequality and we have the violent explosions of Watts or the suppressed and hideous hatreds of Johannesburg. Even without these extremes, it is the universal evidence of all modernizing societies that their urban patterns are bleak, uncreative, obstructive, and even antihuman. In such conditions the quantity of resources may well increase while the actual quality of life declines.

The third problem is a problem of scale. "Demand manage-

ment" has been successfully practiced for over a decade in
what we can call continental economies. But suppose the
economy is not on America's or the new Europe's majestic
scale? Suppose it is a densely populated island economy de-
pendent for 30 percent of its livelihood upon foreign trade?
Suppose it is Britain? What then? There are more small economies than large in our worldwide economic system today, and
we cannot make any very confident prophecies about future
economic directions without looking at the other side of the
economic obstacle race—the growth of the international
economy.

It grew very quickly. Britain, the first power to begin the
technological revolution, was as short of resources as Ricardo
feared—"sitting in coal and surrounded by fish, otherwise
ill-provided," as someone once described the British Isles. But
British capital set off overseas to open up the farms, mines, and
plantations and to build the railways and ports needed to supply food and raw materials for Britain's hungry machines and
mouths. Neighbors in Europe copied the process of industrialization. The New England states, no longer caught in the restrictive patterns of the old colonial control, forged ahead.
Within sixty years, the world was cocooned round with a
thickening web of investment and commercial exchanges, the
ships collecting distant cargoes of wheat from Argentina, palm
oil from the Niger Delta, tea from Calcutta, cotton from the
Southern states, and carrying back to ports or railheads all
round the world the goods and machinery of the new technology.

At the core of the system was Britain's preeminence as investor and provider of industrial goods. Sterling went out in investments and manufactures, came back in Britain's growing purchases of raw materials. This steady pumping through the whole system of the major currency gave a deceptive simplicity to the task of financing the vast new expansion of world commerce. Ultimately debts were settled in gold but, since sterling was always available, gold settlements tended to be marginal. A series of remarkable goldstrikes—in California, in Australia, and then, massively, in South Africa—also helped to offset the possibly restrictive effects of using gold as the working capital of world trade. In that heyday of early expansion, it must have seemed that Adam Smith's generous dream of a free, self-regulating, wealth-creating, worldwide realm of commerce was becoming a fact. The belief that it worked of itself, that you did not have to do anything about it or introduce authorities to guide it and rules to run it, struck deeply into the commercial imagination. Leave it alone, was the cry. The market would do the trick.

But of course it would not. A worldwide system based upon fifty states, numberless dependencies, and millions upon millions of people was just as likely to run into difficulties as the domestic market—indeed, more likely—and would need just the same policies of rational regulation and orderly help. Only, with no authorities above the national level, the process was bound to be much more troublesome. And so, indeed, it has proved to be.

As the world economy developed, it began to show three major factors of imbalance. The British economy was too small to sustain its worldwide role and, with its eclipse, there emerged perpetual difficulties with the world's balance of payments. Europe, divided into small highly self-conscious nations, failed to develop the scale of economy needed for successful growth. The "Third World" of colonial or semicolonial economies outside the Atlantic arena grew patchily or not at all. These three obstructions were at the root of the great crisis of 1929. In possibly a less virulent but still dangerous form, they plague us still. Fully as much as the disproportions of power in our world, these factors of economic disequilibrium threaten to undermine what peace and construction we have achieved and, uncorrected, could pull us back to the anarchy of the first fifty years of this century. But to overcome them decisively demands—as with the problems of power—a readiness to go beyond existing institutions and national restrictions and rethink our world on a new scale. It is by no means clear that we are ready to do so.

No doubt, our worldwide economic system faces other difficulties—for instance, working arrangements with the Communist states. But we are not likely to succeed there unless we have greater stability and coherence in our own half. In fact, the last decade has shown how easily, from the West's point of view, Communist trade can be assimilated to the bounding energetic economies of the Western world. But if they were to fall apart in disunity and decline, the confrontation with Communist pressures could look very different.

These pages are therefore concerned with the difficulties that arise outside the Communist bloc and can, to some extent, be solved without their direct cooperation. To draw them more fully into a productive functioning worldwide economy is, of course, a further aim, but first its functions and its productiveness have to be secured. And from the end of the nineteenth century onwards, it has been clear that the three structural defects already outlined stand in the way of secure growth and full effectiveness.

The British economy was outclassed—by the United States and, up to a point, by Germany—before the end of the nineteenth century. But, by then, it had acquired a vast empire and very large overseas investments. Both masked the passing of effective power which was further whittled away in World War I. But they also shielded Britain from the full consequences of lost supremacy. An overseas income offset a steady decline in the old export industries—in coal, in textiles, in their sales abroad. Victory increased complacency and lessened the political will needed for active modernization and renewal. The country settled down to unemployment and declining industry. True, it went on acting as a world creditor and banker. Sterling continued to be the currency used in about half the world's transactions, but the heart beating behind the old pumping system was no longer strong enough for the task.

The new center of gravity in the world economy—the giant economy of the United States—did not naturally and automatically take over the British role. Once it replaced Britain as the most powerful economic unit in the system, the old self-balancing provision of working capital or "liquidity" for world trade began to break down. American exports included raw materials as well as manufactures. Tariffs protected America's home market. It became more difficult to cover America's growing investments and sales abroad with adequate return sales to America. Between the wars, the warning signals of a dollar shortage appeared and with it a drain of gold across the

Atlantic and a tightening of the working capital available for trade. No large new gold strikes offset the contraction and after 1927 fears of losing still more gold to America was one factor in the slowing down of economic activity in Europe. Equally, an overheated America did not raise interest rates for fear of attracting yet more gold. By 1929, the whole working of the supposedly automatic system of international liquidity—or rather its nonworking—only increased the risk of collapse which, in September of that year, duly began.

Britain's industrial stagnation in the 1920s and 1930s reflected the second structural imbalance in the Atlantic economy—the fact that the new technologies of mass production demanded a scale of markets and resources which most of the old nation-states in Europe did not command and which their enflamed nationalism prevented them from seeking together. This difficulty is fundamental. A whole planetary economy in which men and capital moved freely might in theory have worked out the kind of self-regulating balance by which Adam Smith and his free-trading disciples looked forward. But the Atlantic world in fact was already a world of competing, antagonistic, parochial nation-states. Only the United States, with its continental economy and vast resources, had the elbowroom for growth, for experiments, for mistakes, for success beyond all measure. But Europe's frontiers were too narrow from the start. Britain, by beginning first, had, for a time, the whole world to explore, but the predominance was fleeting. Later entries—France, the Low Countries, above all Germany—felt they could not compete on equal terms with established British industry and decided, as had the Americans, to protect their own nascent industrial system with tariffs high enough to give a strong advantage to local manufacture.

There is, of course, a real dilemma here. If the law of maximum advantage had been followed, the nations of Europe would have risked seeing, so they thought, all the continent's industry concentrated in, say, the British and German coal fields. Modernization might thus have virtually passed them by. This can happen *inside* a national market. Southern Italy still has to catch up with the north. Appalachia has remained on the margin of American prosperity. But at least *within* a state, some wealth is shared from other regions, a central government has some responsibility. *Between* nation-states, no such instruments of wider distribution exist. The alternatives are therefore either to take protective action and set up tariffs at the national level—which may create a completely uneconomic local market—or to join in larger units with some responsibility for industrial location and for some sharing of wealth. Today, the proposed economic unions in East Africa or in Central America face precisely these choices. A hundred years ago, they confronted Europe. The response then was partial and ended by increasing rather than lessening the continent's "tribal" divisions. The German micro-principalities did form a customs union, but what this led to was not the nucleus of a European-wide confederation but a belated German nation-state. The little states of Italy did the same. But by that time, compared with the continental scale of economy needed for the new technology and the new mass markets, they were already too small. The nation-state had been, no doubt, the incubator of the modern economy but incubators are unhandy homes for the full-grown.

By the end of the nineteenth century, nationalist competition for inadequate markets was one factor in revived imperialism and in the drive towards world empire. World War

I, however, left Europe with an even more daunting legacy of competing states. By 1927, the League of Nations was warning the continent that increased protectionism had strangled trade and, unchecked, would produce depression—which duly came two years later, bringing Nazism and renewed war in its wake.

These economies of the North Atlantic, for all their difficulties and contradictions, at least achieved a fairly complete apparatus of modernization in the first two centuries of the technological revolution. But outside this inner Western core— where conditions roughly similar to Britain's have led to similar breakthroughs—the impact of the modern economy has produced more sluggish results. We come now to the third of our structural disproportions—inadequate growth throughout the developing "south." Here colonial and semicolonial economies have been only partially drawn in to the processes of technological change. Western capital—from Britain, then from Europe and North America—flowed in to Asia, to Africa, to Latin America to open up their mines and the land. Lively modernized import-export sectors grew up, the railways and roads and harbors were installed to send out the materials to the North Atlantic states and bring back their manufactures. Nearly all great "southern" cities are seaports. Nearly all their lines of communication run down to the sea—hence the French phrase, *l'economie de traite,* the milch-cow economy.

These special conditions of economic dependence have had two consequences. One is internal. The influence of the modern sector remained restricted. Capital did not accumulate since most of the earnings were despatched overseas. But without credits the institutions needed to encourage and channel savings into investment did not appear, businesses did not spring up in competition with imported manufactures, and virtually no investment occurred in traditional static food-farming, whether it was communal or feudal. Education remained the preserve of a small elite or provided clerks and tally men for the jobs in export trades. In fact, outside this export sector, stimulated from abroad and, in a sense, run as part of the worldwide Atlantic economy, the old order remained, growing, by contrast with more modern ways, not less entrenched but steadily less attractive as time went on.

It is significant that Russia, for all its ancient culture, had touches of this semimodernized, semicolonial condition in 1914—much of its investment in the hands of foreigners, its infrastructure built by them, a very small indigenous industrial class, stagnant agriculture outside the grain exporting areas, deep resentment among the young over the lack of modernity, a crisis of authority, and national identity. Marxist-Leninism in 1917 was simply the catalyst of a crisis already far advanced in violence and contradiction. In China's case, the semicolonial pattern is even clearer—with foreigners in physical control of the ports, internal revenues mortgaged to pay foreign debts, and the country virtually divided into foreign spheres of influence. Communism in these two vast countries came as a kind of theoretical top-dressing for a much more fundamental revolt againt the presence and power of the foreigner, against "colonialist" exploitation, and against the paralysis that seemed to prevent the spread of modernization from its existing meager basis to the rest of the economy.

The second consequence of the derivative quality of "southern" economies is an *external* consequence. The international trade upon which all their pretensions to modernity depend has long been largely beyond their control and directed primarily in other peoples' interests. The organization of the markets for primary products was—and is—in the main under Atlantic control. The tariff structures of international trade have been—often, no doubt, unconsciously—designed to keep the primary producers from developing any local processing. Most of the middleman earnings—from shipping, insurance, banking, the organization of markets—still flow back to the rich Atlantic originators of world trade. Research favors them. Their greater investments tip the balance of new discoveries in their favor. In short, internal contradictions do not end the troubles of the developing "south." They have long been enmeshed in an international trading system which both provides much of what wealth they have, yet is designed to see that its benefits are unequally divided. Significantly, in 1929, the third element in the crisis was the culminating point in a steady decline of primary prices and the collapse of purchasing power throughout the colonial or semicolonial "Third World."

The crisis of 1929 must be regarded as the "moment of truth" for those who believed in a self-functioning, automatic, world economic system rising above the competing interests of an arbitrary number of sovereign nations, each pursuing its own policies in the sublime but silly belief that the self-interest of each would add up to the like-interest of all. The three great imbalances brought the system down. It was in essence, as the late Per Jacobsson, the respected, sagacious, and conservative head of the International Monetary Fund, pointed out, a collapse springing from a failure in effective demand. Our three disproportions were in each case the cause of the failure. Britain's desperate effort to keep for sterling the prestige of a world currency led to the refixing of the value of sterling in gold in 1925. Since the move was to some extent a matter of national pride, sterling was overvalued. As a result, Britain's failing exports became more expensive and failed still more. Its economy sank into further stagnation. The traditional method of reviving it—lower interest rates and hence cheaper credit to stimulate investment—would, it was thought, have sent more capital off to earn more in safe harbor in New York. The world banker's currency might be "good as gold," but his sales and his purchases—on which the vitality of his banking house really depended—continued to shrink, pulling down world demand with them.

But in America, as we have noticed, a rip-roaring boom increased by speculation ought to have been checked sooner by increasing interest rates and making further investment more expensive. But such a move might have emptied worried, unstable Europe of gold. America kept interest rates low, the boom shot ahead, and the final collapse was all the more shattering.

The problem of reserves also played its part in damping down activity inside Europe. By the late 1920s, the overall stimulus to growth given by postwar reconstruction had come to an end. As demand slackened, each individual nation increased both its efforts to sell and its tariff protection against other nations' similar efforts. But this mutual cutting of neighbors' throats effectively checked any *internal* restoration of demand. None of the small European states was self-sufficient. All depended on trade. All had to sell abroad in order to purchase essential supplies. So if they began to increase output, they needed more imports and more exports to pay for them.

Yet if all their neighbors were trying not to buy, their purchases could ultimately be paid for only in gold. So, quite
apart from the risk of a transatlantic hemorrhage, shrinking reserves also inhibited any expansion of activity inside Europe.

To this must be added the third contradictory factor—the
worldwide collapse in primary prices. From the American farm
to the Malayan rubber plantation, incomes from primary
products fell away as activity slackened in the Atlantic economy. Then, in 1929, all the various deflations—in North
America, in Europe, in the world at large—came together.
Purchasing power drained relentlessly and hopelessly out of
the international economy. Between 1929 and 1930, world
trade fell by three-quarters in nine months. As the 1930s began, the economies of the West, beached high above the water
line of demand, looked for all the world like a colony of
stranded whales.

They were as helpless and clumsy in their efforts of recovery. Only a concerted recreation of demand on both sides of
the Atlantic could have reversed the downward rush without
exposing individual governments to impossible pressure on
their reserves. All had to become buyers again if there were to
be any successful revival of selling. But internally governments
did not accept the prime responsibility for launching expansion
on any effective scale. This was still held to be the task of private agencies. Internationally, the nations did meet to consider
joint action—at the World Economic Conference of 1933—but
could agree on nothing, neither diagnosis nor cure. In the
event, one government did violently break the deadlock and
set in motion a vast reexpansion of the economy. But this was
Nazi Germany and its enormous program of "public works"

was all-out preparation for war. Into this, the whole Atlantic world was finally drawn with not one of the basic problems of economic balance solved. It would have taken a bold prophet to predict that in the later half of the century they would be shown to have sunk without trace. And, in fact, each of them, though in somewhat different guise, has resurfaced in the last decade.

Since the end of the war, the Atlantic world has enjoyed its longest and most dynamic period of growth without major setbacks in the whole of its history. Part of the credit goes, of course, to domestic policy—to the tacit or overt agreement of all governments that they cannot afford high unemployment and falling demand. But no amount of sound internal policy-making would work if the international context became unfavorable. Here, too, the three imbalances of earlier Western economic development seem to have been causing much less trouble.

The problem of working capital for world trade and the role of Britain in providing this liquidity does not seem so acute. World trade has grown steadily, in most years by at least 5 percent. Working capital has been adequate for this unprecedented expansion. How has the change come about? One reason lies in the readiness of the nations to set up, after the war, an international instrument in the shape of the International Monetary Fund to oversee their balance of payments and provide temporary financing to tide nations over the fluctuations in their flow of trade. It has worked with increasing effectiveness and growing reserves for nearly two decades. Then, again, although Britain emerged from the war with its overseas investment virtually liquidated and large war debts in their place, it has so far contrived, with considerable outside support, to maintain the balancing act of keeping sterling as an acceptable international currency and continued to help finance a large share in world trade.

But the chief force reversing the old inadequacy and imbalance is, of course, the policy of the United States. America emerged from the war with virtually the Western world's entire gold supply—outside the hands of hoarders. That supply has now, as a result of immensely imaginative and generous policies, been reduced by half. This change has not come about because of any basic change in America's pattern of trade. Each year it sells goods and services abroad worth at least $4,000 millions more than its purchases. But between 1948 and 1952 it gave the West European nations in outright gifts under the Marshall Plan some $13,000 millions with which to rebuild their economies. Since then, it has given enough in aid and supplied enough in investments to run a large and steady deficit in its balance of payments which, in some years, has gone above $3,000 millions. This large outflow of dollars, which can be turned into gold at $35 an ounce on demand, has been used as a reserve currency and has underpinned a considerable part of the world's remarkable expansion in trade.

Now, to turn to the second imbalance—nationalist obstructions in Europe—these too have seemed much less damaging. True, the continent came out of the war with its national divisions, its protectiveness, its strait jacket of would-be self-sufficiency, if anything, increased by the ruin of war. Trade had been about reduced to barter. Foreign reserves had all been lost. The appalling winter of 1947 threatened to give a

deathblow to any hopes of reasonable recovery. It was then
that the United States not only offered the billions of Marshall
money but insisted that Europe act jointly to allocate and use
the funds. This breaking down of barriers sent Western Europe
forward on a collective course. European leaders of the
stature of Schumann and Monnet, of de Gasperi, Spaak, and
Adenauer, carried on the momentum, and the dream of a Europe
rising above its old parochial limitations took shape in the
institutions of the European Community.

Nor was the third area of obstruction—the poverty-striken
"south"—forgotten. Britain passed on much of its Marshall aid
to the Indian subcontinent by releasing sterling to meet war
claims and debts. France began its generous granting of
massive subsidies to Africa. The old colonial policy of each dependency
paying its own way and earning its own keep—a
policy that condemned them to almost complete stagnation
whenever primary prices fell—gave way to a new concept of
assistance for development and metropolitan investment in
such local preconditions of self-help as education, improved
health, better transport, and more power. In 1949, the United
States began direct participation in foreign aid with its Point
Four programs and since then American aid to the "south" has
grown—in some years more, in some less, but now fluctuating
about a figure of some $2,000 millions in economic aid, with
another billion for military support.

There can be no doubt that the phenomenal prosperity of
the Atlantic world since 1947 has been largely based on this
reversal of the old fatalities. Purchasing power has been
maintained—by internal stability, by adequate reserves, by a
widening, growing European market, by investment in the de-

veloping lands. The contrast with the 1920s and 1930s is astonishing and suggests that the international economy, like the
domestic markets of the West, has found a way through its obstructions and obstacles, and, at the world level, too, policies
soundly based for the maintenance and expansion of effective
demand are being successfully evolved.

But no hats should be sent up in the air. The rejoicing could
be premature. Although each of the three solutions points towards a new kind of genuine postnational method of running
human affairs, the breakthrough is not complete. The solutions
have depended, and up to a point still do depend, upon American generosity, leadership, and predominance—in other
words, still on the policies of a single nation-state. This fact in
turn aggravates a second. In spite of the world's stunning experience of the horrors perpetrated in the name of nationalist
mania during the war, the old phobias are stirring again. And
naturally day by day, hour by hour, American national predominance tends to irritate the potential nationalism of everybody else.

The issue of working capital for trade is bedeviled by the
clash between American national policy and Europe's revived
sense of its own economic strength. The French lead a solid
body of European opinion in wanting a change from the last
decade's primary dependence upon the dollar. They have genuine grievances, for instance, the tendency of American investment to be used to buy up French and other European businesses. So long, the critics say, as dollars are not converted into
gold but are banked away instead as a reserve currency, Europeans are, in effect, lending America the dollars with which to
secure control of their economy. Moreover, the influx of dollars

increases a source of demand over which governments have no control and which may counteract their attempts to control the tide of inflation. But there is another possibly deeper reason— nationalist resentment at the economic predominance of the United States and the consequent desire to expell the dollar from service as a general reserve. General de Gaulle has therefore proposed that gold be restored as the sole component of international reserves and the dollar return to its original status as simple American currency. His more conservative advisers suggest than any shortage of liquidity created by these means can be offset by increasing the price of gold.

The General's position is at one extreme. At the other is the belief of many Americans that the dollar is "good as gold" and should remain the pivot of world liquidity. They, too, have some reason on their side. They point out that gold is a yardstick of value rather than useful in itself. No system can be stable if the yardstick is unstable. Raise the price of gold now and you encourage every worthless speculator to continue his sterile game, you give an unearned bonus to the most illiberal state in the world—South Africa (not to speak of the Soviets) —and you leave yourself with nothing but the certainty of further price rises, further uncertainty, and hence sustained speculation when in the future gold output diminishes, reefs run out, yet world trade has to continue to grow. So, the extreme American advocates argue, get out of the bullion business now. Let the dollar carry on as the chief reserve currency as effectively as it has done for the last decade. After all, what people want from a reserve is the ultimate ability to buy food, materials, and machines. Name anything the dollar will not buy.

What are we to say of this apparent deadlock? The first is

that it is insoluble in purely national terms. To go back to the uncontrolled working of a gold standard based on the individual policies of single sovereign states is to return to the incoherence of the past. The United States has only to bring its trade back into balance, France has only to renew its love affair with gold, and the world economy will be heading for precisely the rocks that wrecked it between the wars. The liquidity issue can be settled only by moving forward to a genuine international agreement from which, hopefully, the elements of national prestige, adolescent arrogance and atavistic resentment have been banished. And, to judge by the successful functioning of the credit system *within* the national economy, the solution lies somewhere between the extremes of the European and American positions.

To go back to gold would be about as sensible as to return to bullion in the internal banking system. *Credit* has been the chief basis of the unparalleled expansion of internal production. The gold base is no more than a yardstick. The real values are the goods and materials, at predictable prices, which the system produces. Any system that obscures that reality weakens the rationality of the whole international economy.

Equally, no developed domestic economy would function well if all the credit were provided by no more than a couple of banks. The Chase Manhattan and the First National City could hardly provide America with a secure credit system singlehanded. In order to consolidate and expand the whole business of lending and base it on the strength of the whole economy, the country requires its Federal Reserve system. The dollar and sterling are, as it were, single banks, and the solution needed for the world economy is to get away from reserves based on a couple of individual countries and transform the International Monetary Fund into a global reserve system in which the expanding credit for trade is issued on the basis of the output and productivity of *all* the national economies—on marks and francs as well as dollars and sterling—and is underpinned by the rising wealth of the whole world economy. Lord Keynes' concept of "bancor" as a unit of credit issued by the IMF is one version of such a scheme. The idea of the "CRU" put forward by the more moderate wing in France can be expanded to serve the same function. Of course, such a policy entails handing over to the IMF considerable control over liquidity and credit creation. As an essential preliminary, Britain's large foreign debt would need to be funded, and the United States would need to bring its deficit under control. All the trading nations would have to accept the discipline of running neither persistent deficits nor persistent surpluses. The working capital needed over and above the regular movement of reserves in response to trade debts and surpluses could then be provided in an orderly fashion through the judicious creation of credit by the IMF. The essential point is to achieve a cooperative post-nationalist solution which gets away from the pretensions and strains aroused by the use of individual currencies and resembles as much as possible the successful impersonal working of the credit system *inside* the developed economy.

A similar tangle of mixed nationalist motives and resentments confuses the advance towards a more workable Europe. Its most tragic aspect has been the falling out of Anglo-Saxon and Gaul. The story begins with Britain's postwar combination of weakness and illusion. For ten years after the end of the Marshall Plan, the British clung to their old imperial vision of

themselves as a separate Great Power with worldwide responsibilities. In spite of the amount of shoring-up from outside
their shaky economy required—a $3,000 millions American
loan immediately after the war, loans from Canada, some hid-
den subsidies from such dollar-earners as Malaya or the Gold
Coast spirited in through the operations of the sterling area,
the massive assistance of the Marshall Plan, and, lately, a couple of $1,000 millions rescue operations mounted through the
IMF—the country behaved as though its old position was intact and continued to maintain the increasingly expensive traditional role of banker-cum-policeman all round the world.

This burden could perhaps have been carried if a thorough
reorganization of Britain's industrial system and habits of management and work had been carried out at the same time.
Some modernization, of course, did occur and exports rose—
but at a much slower rate than that of expanding world trade.
To give only the most recent figures for the mid-1960s, while
world trade increased by 10 percent in 1963/64, British exports
to industrial countries rose by only 5 percent, while their exports to Britain rose by over 20 percent. Unhappily, the repeated economic shoring-up from outside had blunted the
sense in Britain of needing drastic change. Its world role had
also entailed a lot of passing on of the funds received. A sort of
shadow play of empire went on while the reality of strength
waned further still.

This shadow play was the cause of Britain's most disastrous
single decision—not to be associated, once the pressure of the
Marshall Plan was over, with the work of European unity.
No doubt, in terms of historical experience as well as continuing tribalism, the decision was all but inevitable. The British

had almost learnt to be a nation by disliking the French. Shakespeare's most noble verse celebrates the island's separateness—the gem set in a silver sea and moated "against the envy of less happier lands." Its greatness *had* seemed to lie in a world-ranging escape from Europe, its memories to dwell on distances spanning "palm and pine" across the open sea. "We happy few" had enjoyed the country's finest hour in 1940 when, significantly, the island was absolutely alone and enjoyed it.

But all this is the rhetoric of national life. The bread-and-butter facts are of two world wars fought because competing nationalisms are not a base either for order or for prosperity in a modern continent. After 1945, Britain either joined in the movement to create a post-national order, or it prepared the way for the old collapse. The choice to stay out was doubly disastrous. It was tragic for Britain meandering on in its fading dreams of great powerhood, but tragic for Europe where the British talents for good administration, common-sense politics, liberal manners, and a worldwide vision would have vastly reinforced the new moderation and rationality of politics after the Gothic horrors of the Fascist years.

By the time the brilliant success of the Common Market in expanding trade and maintaining growth rates of 4 and 5 percent a year on the continent—compared with Britain's 2½ percent—had convinced some of the country's leaders that the British had better leave their dream of national sufficiency and after all climb on the European gravy train, another set of nationalist illusions had found a leader and reached a pitch that made possible the stinging rebuff which excluded Britain from the Community early in 1963.

With General de Gaulle, we reach a deeper pathology—an addiction of the whole being to the national idea. It is understandable. France's war record had no "finest hour." The postwar period, from the national point of view, was one of disastrous colonial defeat and humiliating dependence upon a moralizing, anticolonial, intolerably wealthy United States. The General was not very well handled by the two "Anglo-Saxons," Churchill and Roosevelt, and that he owed his emergence to them was hardly likely to endear them further.

But dislike of past humiliations at the hands of the British and the Americans is not the root of the matter. General de Gaulle simply believes in the nation. The mystic sense of *la patrie* breathes through all his writings. Had he been in power he would almost certainly have neither signed the Treaty of Rome nor participated in the supranational experiments that led up to it. He has tolerated it since his return to power in 1958 for only two reasons. Its economic basis, a bargain struck between the French farmer and the German industrialist, enables him to cope with the rising productivity of French farms and sell inside the protected market the awkward surpluses which otherwise tend to be spread by angry peasants on the roads of France. Its political justification is the degree to which it gives him the hope of substituting French for American leadership in Europe and is a base from which "to throw the (American) rascals out."

But if the Community is destined to grow into a genuine European state-system on, presumably, a federal basis, he will have none of it. This is the critical point the Community has reached today. The bargain in agriculture, by which levies against foreign farm produce are used to prevent competition with internal, largely French supplies, has already conferred considerable financial powers on the European Commissioners in Brussels since they are to collect and redistribute the levies. When the Commission proposed that all customs receipts, including not only the levies but tariffs on industrial goods as well, should be centrally administered, General de Gaulle withdrew all senior French representation and left the organization to await his next move of displeasure. His reason was simple. In 1913, the federal income of the United States was still largely composed only of customs receipts. Yet it was enough to underpin a flourishing federation. The General sees the centralization of Community income as a commitment to federalism, to supranational order, to the organization of Europe on post-national lines. He will not accept it. He prefers the old weary run of Europe's war-ridden nationalist past.

In these circumstances, it may be that the believers in Europe have now to mark time—whether they be Dutch or Belgian or German or Italian, or, indeed, those Frenchmen who have so ingeniously worked with M. Jean Monnet to elaborate the experiment in the first place. The next step towards unity may have to wait the passing from power of a very great man who is also a very great anachronism. Meanwhile, the essential need is to hold the Community intact and keep the hope of future unity alive.

Here "the Anglo Saxons" have a part to play. The British could enormously strengthen the will to unity in Europe by announcing their determination to join fully and unequivocally in a European union, to play their full part in developing it along liberal democratic and outwardlooking lines, to join in all its ramifications—for defense as well as for prosperity—and

to seek for it a separate vocation as a federal, continental
power firmly anchored in the world of freedom and ready to
cooperate closely with both its Russian and American neighbors.

The United States, too, has a role but possibly a less ob-
trusive one. In a sense the challenge of nationalism is America's most subtle danger. The country is so obviously the leader.
It has the continental economy equal to all its tasks. It can almost dream of self-sufficiency for it almost has it. If nationalism were an answer to the world's dilemmas, America could
claim to be the proof. But it is not. Liquidity, trade, the growth
of the world market, aid to the "south"—all these need more
than American efforts and America therefore needs friends and
partners. But the role of an elephant cooperating loyally with a
family of cats is never easy. Affection quite as much as anger
can produce disaster. For this reason, to be large and loved is
notoriously difficult. Nineteenth-century Britishers were always
being hurt by what they felt was the lack of gratitude felt by
foreigners for Britain's patently benevolent interfering. Queen
Victoria, in particular, never ceased to lament the world's failure to give thanks.

In this century, America faces the challenge of doing good
by stealth, and certainly the record of the last decades in both
benevolence and lack of fanfare have been notable, especially
at the level of government. The initiative needed now, without
any suggestion of interference or talk of "leadership," is to convey to Europe—even though General de Gaulle may be beyond conviction—America's settled conviction (which first was
proved by the Marshall Plan) that the consolidation of a

strong Europe is in everyone's best interests, that the United States will not try to run it or seek undue favors from it or preferential treatment in it (not even for chickens) or use it as an instrument of the Cold War or any other political purpose. But America will cooperate loyally on all those issues— liquidity or the continuous widening of opportunities for trade or negotiated tariff reductions or worldwide economic assistance or the critical issue of defense—which not even a continent as unified and powerful as the United States can handle alone. If incidentally some restraint on direct investment by giant American corporations in companies in Europe can be shown to increase the sense of the United States' disinterestedness, it might be politically wise. It could also serve the economic purpose of lessening the exodus of dollars. But this is not a major point. The chief need is to convey that sense of equal partnership which Europeans, after the dependence of the last decades, long to feel. True, they have to earn it but it will be helpful if America feels it too.

We are left with the third obstacle to the growth of coherent world economy—the relative stagnation and poverty of the developing south. Here, too, as with the issue of liquidity, some of the most hopeful analogies for action can be drawn from the domestic economy. But here, too, there are national obstacles to the evolution of any such policies. Obstructive nationalism on the side of the recipients can be seen in the extreme difficulty they experience in coming together in the kind of wider economic association that made the Marshall Plan successful. Venezuela continues to refuse membership in Latin America's incipient free-trade area. In Africa, the East African Common Market splits apart and, so far, any solid West African agreement on unified economic policies has proved impossible.

On the side of the donors, the difficulty of concerting and timing joint policies for either aid or trade directly affects their scale and generosity. True, a Development Assistance Committee has been set up under the OECD in Paris but it exercises little authority. Yet in many areas, only joint policies will allow for more liberal trade or a real effort of investment. It is difficult for a nation acting singly to raise prices for primary products, or to relax its restrictions, or reduce tariffs, if its neighbors do nothing of the kind. Then its balance of payments and its domestic market have to take the full effect of the flooding in of, say, cheap textiles or overpriced coffee. True, the expedient of tying aid to purchases bought only from the donor country protects the balance of payments but it has undesirable by-products. It allows a great deal of high-cost goods to be handed on in the name of aid and has, in fact, greatly increased the developing nations' indebtedness. It is also true that separate, uncoordinated efforts are not impossible. The French, for instance, have given special privileges to their African territories—higher prices, guaranteed markets—possibly earning some compensation in countersales of French goods. But even they are moving away from such preferences and have also brought in the other members of the Common Market to share the burden of aid. If the approach were extended to a general Atlantic strategy, there could be more energy, more coherence and less overlapping in the whole effort. Such an attempt would also have the incidental effect of quietening any suggestion that the Powers are using aid programs to create neo-colonialist client states. This criticism is leveled both at French policy in Africa and American policy in Latin America.

However, these manifestations of "going it alone" in policies of assistance are perhaps less disturbing than another type of national mood among the rich nations. This is a certain disillusion with the whole ability of poor nations to make use of the aid they have been given. Some disappointment was perhaps inevitable. The first euphoria of successful assistance achieved through the Marshall Plan rather filled the Atlantic imagination with pictures of smiling, grateful countries taking off into economic orbit with swift and predictable precision. The actual facts of delays, difficulties, disappointments, political "unreliability," and a certain steady unreadiness to show gratitude have blunted the first expectations and induced some cynicism and a considerable loss of confidence.

But this is not the first time that richer people have felt gloomy about the prospects of their poor neighbors. We can recall all the gloom of the Victorian period. So much of what was said then about the poorer classes can be reproduced now in the context of the poor nations. The responsibility of families who have more children when they should be learning thrift, the danger of educating people who then become insubordinate and "above themselves," the hopelessness of giving machines to workers who take the tractors out duck-shooting—a modern equivalent of "coals in the bath"—all the old fears and questions reappear, all the doubts whether anything worthwhile can be done with the mass of proletarians at the bottom of the heap.

But one of the advantages of looking back with a hundred

years' hindsight at that old proletarian world, at, say, the
monstrous London slums painted by Dickens in all their dirt,
despair, and squalor, is to be able to see how enormously
transformable these same proletarians have proved to be and
also to see the steps by which the changes have been accomplished. The differences between the rough migrant "navvies"
who built Britain's first railways or the starving Irish laborers
pouring into English ports and the new proletariat of Asia and
Africa are not so total that one can argue, *a priori,* that similar
policies of rehabilitation and encouragement will not work.

We have already looked at these transformations *within* the
national economy but it may be useful to recall them briefly.
Some of the answer lay in self-help—the combination of ambition and self-respect led to smaller families and a passion for
education and self-improvement. Self-help also took the form
of tough, vigorous action to set up trade unions to organize
parties, to build workers' cooperatives and peasant leagues.
This action in turn helped to alter the distribution of wealth in
the market economy. Trade unions, organized for bargaining,
discovered that the tendency of wages to fall to subsistence
was not a law of nature but a law of man. Once workers could
defend themselves, it was found that the new industrial system
produced enough wealth to permit a lot more of it to come
their way. Besides, enlightened management was shrewd
enough to see first the advantage of a steady, self-respecting
working force—which implies good wages—and later to
realize, with Henry Ford, that a high wage economy is also a
high consumption economy, and good pay implies good sales.
That those who will not buy cannot sell applies to the domestic
wage bargain as fully as to international trade. The total effect

was an enlargement of the market and an expansion of demand from which the whole community could benefit.

The other great aspect of the general improvement lay in direct transfers of wealth from rich to poor by way of the tax system. These taxes financed education, built houses, improved health, bettered urban conditions. They helped the mass of the people to get a more effective start in life and at the same time upgraded the skills of the whole population. If, as modern economists reckon, more than half the increases in the productivity of the last half century have come from better-trained minds, this massive effort of education, much of it underpinned by tax money, must be counted one of the chief levers of general affluence.

Self-help, better shares in production, assistance through taxation—here are three ways in which the downtrodden proletarian classes of the nineteenth century became the fine upstanding consumers of the twentieth. A comparable transition can be achieved for the proletarian nations—provided similar policies are pursued and similar time, at least half a century, is allowed for the change.

The signs of active self-help among the developing nations are not wanting. To take two of the prime Victorian examples —family size and education—the last five years have brought a wholly new emphasis on the nations' responsibility to control the upward surge of population. In two of the largest developing countries—India and Pakistan—both governments are on the verge of massive campaigns to bring families to a manageable size, increase the mothers' health, and give some hope of education and well-being for the children. Given greater knowledge of techniques for controlling fertility and the undoubted fact that two wholly different cultures—Europe and Japan—experienced falling birthrates once modernization took hold, it is possible that twenty years from now not so much the problems of absolute control but the social and cultural implications of smaller families, the role of women, adolescent discipline, relations between the sexes, will take up more of the time and concern of society.

Meanwhile, the new awareness of population problems is more than equaled by an absolute passion for the spread of education. The fisherboy by his net deep in *Junior Mathematics* is the symbol of Africa's hunger for advance. In some developing countries, budgets for education reach 50 percent of public expenditure. The results are not always balanced in terms of available jobs. But no one can doubt the passion for self-help.

Self-help on a wider front is also beginning. The first of seventy-seven developing nations formed after the U.N. Conference on Trade and Development in 1964 can be a most valuable pressure group if it holds together and provides a reasonable and realistic policy. The developed nations, like enlightened employers, should welcome such a potentially strong and responsible "union" and work for the concrete policies which, by increasing the poor nations' share in world prosperity, also improve them as market prospects. In this way the concept of "sustained demand" can begin to be transferred to the world economy and "demand management" become one of its responsibilities and techniques.

Under this heading of wider purchasing power for the poor nations come such possibilities as the reduction of quotas and the revision of tariff structures in the developed north to encourage the processing of local raw materials in the south. It includes the repeal of excise tax on tropical products and steps to secure higher and steadier prices for primary products. It includes policies to secure a larger share in the middleman profits which flow from trade—in shipping, for instance, 94 percent of which is run by the "north," or in insurance where the percentage is nearer 100 percent. On the side of investment, it can cover larger participation by local governments, banks, and investors in foreign enterprises established in the "south." Such steps could help to edge up the share of the "south" in world trade—visible and invisible—to rather more than the present 26 percent—a percentage incidentally which has actually fallen since the early 1950s.

Another method of increasing the developing peoples' stake could lie in some imaginative scheme of compensatory finance. At present, income from primary prices may fluctuate by as much as 15 percent a year—an instability which makes forward planning intensely difficult. If nothing offsets these fluctuations, the wealthy "north" gets the full advantage of falling prices and the southern farmer or miner pays the price.

If, however, the poor nations' needs for compensatory finance to offset fluctuating income were linked to the developed nations' need for liquidity in world trade, it might be possible to evolve a scheme in which part at least of the world's reserves were provided not by gold nor by currencies but by some controlled creation of credit on the part of the world's embryonic central bank, the International Monetary Fund. If each year it were empowered to issue credit certificates to the value, say, of 5 percent of world trade, and these were placed with the near-liquid assets of the World Bank, the Bank could then transfer an equivalent amount of capital to its subsidiary, the International Development Association, for investment in the developing world. Alternatively to make such a proposal respectable to banking opinion, it could follow the French suggestion that the new credit issued by the IMF should be given to the developed nations in the proportion to which they give aid to the underdeveloped. In either case the extra credit would stimulate the growth of trade, and the extra purchasing power, guaranteed by the productive power of the whole world economy, would be issued first to the nations in the greatest need and would quickly pass to the general community. It would be spent on the machines and materials of development, largely available in the "north." It would also at this stage have to be used quite extensively to repay southern debt which between 1956 and 1964 has risen from $7,981 millions to $24,804 millions. Some mitigation of this appalling burden will have to be considered, whatever the solutions for liquidity.

Compensatory finance bridges the gap between trade and aid. And when we turn to aid, we can see again useful analogies with the domestic economy. Inside the nation, the distinction is clear and well understood between domestic assistance programs which simply tide families over temporary disaster —a break in employment, sickness—and those which are designed to give people the regular opportunity—or perhaps a new chance—to make a better life by their own efforts. All education belongs to this category and all the increasing emphasis on it in a dynamic society where higher skills are increasingly needed. So does a lot of expenditure on housing and health. And as it becomes clear that in a rapidly evolving economy, some areas and hence some people get left behind, other forms of direct assistance cover retraining for new jobs, area redevelopment, stimulus to new industry, and so forth.

Now it is clear that although some foreign aid, particularly in food, belongs to the category of relief, the great bulk of aid is aimed at the kind of transformations of skill and opportunity which hopefully flow from money invested in education or in regional renewal or in the whole range of policies included under America's domestic "war on poverty." In a sense, the "south" is a vast Appalachia, an infinitely larger version of Italy's retarded *Mezzogiorno*, an area in which, owing to the unplanned movements of a whole world economy, millions upon millions of people have been left behind. It needs, therefore, some exceptional help in order to catch up.

The pattern of stagnation in this wide area has already been described in broad categories—overdependence on an export sector (which is itself shaky and fluctuating), lack of industry, static agriculture, shortage of credit and the institutions of credit, lack of skills, above all, of entrepreneurial skills; these are in general terms the deficiencies which a judicious combination of self-help, aid, technical assistance, compensatory finance, and better conditions of trade could combine to put right. What any particular country will need in the way of policy and assistance can be decided only after careful study of the local conditions. In most countries in Africa, the first need is for massive assistance to education, particularly secondary education and quick support for an inadequate administrative structure. An almost equal need is for the grouping of the small micro-markets into regions large enough to support any growth at all.

In other areas—one thinks of parts of Latin America—large-scale aid, to be effective, has to wait on institutional change. Agriculture is likely to remain stagnant until the kind of land reform carried out under the Meiji revolution in Japan has been achieved. And until it is, there will be little opening for agricultural investment and not much to be gained by investment in industry either since a stagnant countryside deprives the city of its natural markets.

In India and Pakistan, the largest and most populous of the developing lands outside China, there is enough education and administration and probably just enough development in the countryside to make massive transfers of capital the most effective method of assistance. In both countries, a very considerable infrastructure of transport and power has been built. A sizable industrial sector has come into existence. But the sheer weight of unfavorable factors in foreign trade—Western quotas against textiles, sluggish prices for primary products like tea, jute, and cotton, hard competition from other Asian exporters of manufactures—has prevented much buoyancy in export sales. Foreign exchange for materials and maintenance cannot be fully provided. Factories work below capacity. Unemployment goes up. It is here that massive aid on the Marshall scale could bring astonishingly rapid returns. But the two nations, far from cooperating, have found no solution for their Kashmir dispute. So long as they continue in violent enmity, one can hardly hope for a Marshall spirit in the West. Worse still, the Kashmir tragedy reinforces the skepticism entrenched Western critics already feel about the general effectiveness of aid. The result could be a fall in assistance or, at the least, a continuance of the present stagnation.

Since Western aid reached a plateau of between $8 and $9 billions in 1960/61, there has been no further increase, while

Western GNP has risen by 4 to 5 percent a year. In proportionate terms, Western aid is on the decline. There is, of course, no economic reason for this falling off. If America, in the late 1940s, with a GNP at least one-third smaller than it enjoys today, could put 2 percent of it into the Marshall Plan, the present percentage of roughly 0.5 percent of GNP for aid can hardly be called a burden. After all, the Atlantic powers carry an annual arms effort of some $80,000 million which, far from crippling them, is a source of stimulus to heavy industry and to the whole economy. In 1965, their combined national incomes passed the million million dollar mark. An aid effort of some $9,000 millions can barely be felt—except politically. The American share represents not much more than 10 percent of the country's *annual* increase in wealth. As such, it demands no more than a willingness to grow richer a little more slowly between Christmas and Easter, a not inappropriate gesture for a self-styled Christian country in a season which includes Lent.

No—the difficulties are not economic. At this point we have to register the weakness of all analogies between the success of strategies for growth, stability, and greater distributive justice *inside* Western society and the possible application of similar policies in the world at large. Our larger world society lacks the institutions of unity and it lacks the political will. Inside the modernized state, the pressure of trade unions, the lobbies of the voters, the enlightenment of management, the protest of Christian conscience, all these pressures, organized or inchoate, can focus on centers of effective decision-making at the level of city and region, ultimately at the level of national government.

In our growing, increasingly interdependent international society, there is nothing beyond the level of the nation-state except the fluctuating activity derived from bargaining and treaty-making of powers which can and will withdraw what they have given and reverse their pledged undertaking. One dissenting French partner can put the European Commission on to a care-and-maintenance basis. The OECD has barely even advisory powers. Every U.N. organ—from the Security Council to each Specialized Agency—is a bargaining center and in spite of the very real and independent authority achieved by such effective agencies as the World Bank or the International Monetary Fund, they can only hope to influence their national directors. They cannot command their support. The final decisions lie with the bargain-makers at the national level. All this means that the hard, surviving centers of decision are still the nations. In spite of all their inadequacies as instruments of either security or abundance, they have not relinquished their claim. Everything above the national level, however necessary, however beneficial, can still be revoked, except, of course, reality itself.

And this tough survival of sovereignty no doubt reflects the continued dominance among men of a parochial or tribal political will. The focus of unforced, spontaneous cohesion is still the community of the nation-state. Even where it does not yet exist, its creation is the first concern of government. Where it has deep foundations, it has emerged, rocklike, above the receding floods of ideology. There is still no profound sense of emotional commitment or community in the larger society of man. To the gaps in power and the gaps in wealth, we have to add the profound moral and emotional gaps that exist in a world of infinitely divided loyalties. It is possible that these are the most divisive and dangerous of all.

FOUR

The Balance of Ideology

For a decade or so after the war, it was possible, indeed, it was natural, to feel that the ideological divisions of the Cold War made a more cooperative world order inconceivable. There, on one side of the Iron Curtain, were the hordes of atheistic Communism; here, on our side, stood the free defenders of Western civilization. In 1949, the sense of defending a beleaguered freedom grew more intense when China fell to the Communists. Moscow and Peking forged an ideological alliance and began to step up the campaign of anti-Western subversion and propaganda among the developing nations. Thus a global struggle to defend freedom against expansive Communism almost inevitably dominated the Western world-picture of the 1950s.

But in the 1960s the clear lines of this picture have smudged a little at the edges. Unmistakably, all round the world, another force—also in a sense an ideological force but of a different kind—has clouded the Cold War quarrels and suggested that perhaps after all they are not what divides men most. This force is old-fashioned nationalism, the traditional assertion of separate national identity, the automatic preference of one part of earth to any other, the instinctive readiness to believe that rights, obligations, and at times even courtesy and mercy naturally and self-evidently cease at this seashore or that river line. General de Gaulle disrupts Europe's nascent attempts at unity simply because "it is inadmissible that outside interests should determine France's economic destiny." Herr Strauss ominously tries to revive in Germany the memories of second-class nationhood imposed at Versailles. In Eastern Europe, Rumania accuses its Communist neighbors of trying to check its industrial growth as a nation. Across the long Asian borders of Russia, China raises the issue of "unequal treaties" and hints at the return of territories filched from China by the czars. None of this has anything to do with the Cold War. Indeed, one of the gravest Asian crises since 1945—Kashmir—is a simple projection of unsettled frontiers and national claims.

Should we be surprised? If we take a long enough view of history, the answer clearly is "No." Communism is in a sense a crusading religion and throughout the human record, such religions have swept out to conquer territories, sometimes creating a single authority, but then have ebbed or settled down, while preexistent boundaries and authorities reappear above the flood. Many of the communities which existed in conscious statehood before the Muslim tide of conquest in the seventh and eighth centuries reemerged afterwards and can be counted to this day all along the Mediterranean and on to the frontiers of India.

But in the case of Communism there is a deeper reason why its dispute with the free societies of Western Europe and the Atlantic may not prove to be a final obstacle to more cooperative relations. However divided the two systems appear on the surface, they have their roots in the same cultural revolution and are twin aspects of the most remarkable cultural conquest ever experienced by man—the conquest of the whole world by the restless dynamic spirit of the West.

For most of its millennial history, mankind has not lived in a dynamic society. In fact, it is the very last kind of society it would have chosen. A strong human preference for the safe, the stable, the predictable, and therefore the repetitive seems to have lasted for some hundred millennia. Only during the last two or three hundred years have whole societies begun to seek the opposite principle of dynamic change.

In tribal life—the longest by thousands of years of any human experiment—communal unity leaves the individual with no very acute sense of his own separateness. Authority is based on kinship and age, not on achievement. Work is communal. Property—the means of work—is communal. Work and worship are barely distinguished for the right agricultural practices are also a consecrated ritual which must not be changed for fear of inviting the displeasure of extra-human forces. This is not to say that tribal life was without storms. Failures of harvests and hunting grounds led to treks and wars. At the very earliest stage of human organization, we encounter aggression and conquest as a condition of survival for one group and of potential extinction for its neighbor. But, short of ultimate disaster, tribal society tended to cope with its disorders without breaking unity, conformity, and tradition.

The same fixed stars shine over the next phase of human development. The great archaic civilizations which grew up on the Nile or the Euphrates or the Indus or the Yellow rivers were, of course, infinitely more elaborate. The vast cooperative, coordinated efforts needed to control great flows of water broke up the old simplicities of work and property. Specialization increased output and scope and led to much more differentiated types of human activity. Some men were the treasurers and planners, some the guardians, some the farmers, some the boatmen. Thus was created a hierarchy of jobs with the least pleasant left to the least privileged, who were usually slaves.

The men of power—the priests who could influence fate, interpret signs, and, in time, decipher script, the soldiers with command in the field, the ruler who often combined all three functions—demanded a higher reward and, since land was the largest source of wealth, land revenues were attached to temples and courts to provide rewards and costs of administration. Lands also slipped from tribal ownership to the control of tribal chiefs on their way to becoming territorial lords. As late as the 1940s, one could still virtually see the process at work in Iraq as local leaders used the process of registering land titles as a cover for the transfer of communal lands to their own use.

The result of these profound changes in archaic civilization was a much more wealthy order of society but one in which man, cast out from the poverty-stricken paradise of shared communal work and reward, began to face an inescapable hierarchy of wealth, prestige, and opportunity, and began to experience the alienation of man from man.

This whole issue of human rewards and privileges can be settled equitably, it seems, only at each end of the scale of wealth. The tribe where all share the same poverty is not riven with class resentment. The struggles and rivalries for resources

look outwards, against other tribes' forests, reserves, and fishing rivers. Possibly the modern technological society can provide a middle-class standard for virtually all its members. But
in between, over the millennia, the history of the great mass of
the people seems only to have been a series of variations on the
single themes of work, shortage, and injustice.

Instruments of social unity were thus even more necessary
than in the old communal societies. Profound obedience on the
part of the subject secured by fixing divine and royal authority,
profound adherence to traditional habits in thought, in patterns of work and administration, profound acceptance of orderly recurrence as the will of God or destiny—these were the
underpinning of the elaborate, splendid, and unequal societies.
The whole of creation was drawn in to confirm and illustrate
this profound and conservative bias against innovation and unpredictable change. Man's cycle of life from birth to death, the
return of the seasons, stars wheeling in the firmament, the pas-
sage of the years all point to a revolving reality perpetually re-
newing the same patterns. Thus they demand from man, as the
highest wisdom, the mood of acceptance and resignation. These
are the great underlying certainties of human fate in archaic
civilization. Whether the outward form is the hieratic splendor
of the first kings of Babylonia or the Yellow Emperor dedicating
the Chinese empire to the Way of Heaven, or Egyptian dynasties preserving their stupendous cult of death intact over thousands of years, the inner meaning is order, recurrence, tradition, and conformity.

The vast, magnificent, and internally static systems spanned
the world in the millennia before Christ. Indeed, we should
not forget that outside Western Europe they remained the

outer form of human civilization until only three or four hundred years ago. In China, desperate efforts were still being made to preserve their forms in the middle of the nineteenth century. By any ordinary historical calculation, no doubt, they should have set the pattern for the future. But, then, no one would have foreseen the hominid in the days of the dinosaur, and the growing points for the future lay not with the great empires but with two small peoples of genius in the Eastern Mediterranean—the Greeks and the Jews—whose cultures, fused, modified, and transmitted through Western Christendom, provide the context of our modern society.

The degree to which these traditions diverge from older concepts of human order has often been described. Here I only want to pick out the basic elements in the swing from a static to a dynamic view of man and his destiny, for this, in essence, is what the emergence of Western civilization means. Man ceases to be subject and slave with conformity as his highest social virtue. For the Greeks, he is a citizen who is free because he lives under laws he helps to frame. For the Jews he is a free moral person since he can choose or not to act out a God-given destiny. The incurious acceptance of traditional wisdom grows weaker in both cultures and we can see the early stirrings of the scientific spirit in the Greek intoxication with reason and with the harmonies of mathematical and musical law, the Jewish sense of the value and importance of material things in God's creation—"The beasts of the fields are mine and mine are the cattle upon a thousand hills." It is surely no coincidence that two great archetypal figures in both traditions are symbols of man's insatiable curiosity—Prometheus stealing the fire of the gods, Job rejecting all trite or moralizing consolations for his agony and challenging God Himself to give it meaning.

But it is above all to the Jews that we owe the two uniquely dynamic elements in the Western tradition. The first is the total break with the concept of history as repetition. Living after so many centuries of Western thought, we find it difficult to realize how at variance the idea of progress is with the repetitive physical realities of the day-to-day world. Nearly everything *is* cyclical. Nearly everything has a cycle of growth and decay. It takes the boldest, the most audacious leap of imagination to make a complete break with such overwhelming practical evidence and instead see history as the unfolding of a divine purpose, as the progressive revelation of God's will for man which will be realized in the measure of man's free response. Since so much of what we see depends upon the kind of ideas we bring to our observation, it is quite possible that the whole evidence of man's evolutionary ascent from the original amoeba could only have been discovered in a society which had already acquired a sense of progress and unfolding purpose from quite another source.

When we ask what kind of progress and purpose the Jewish vision entailed, we come to the second unique element of dynamism. The vision is profoundly concerned with man's social existence here and now. What is hoped for is "the *coming* of the Kingdom," and one of the profound marks of this kingdom will be an end to social inequalities and injustice and the recovery of primal brotherliness and goodwill. "He has put down the mighty from their seats and exalted them of low degree."

The note sounds, I believe, in no other culture. Poverty is among the evils which some Eastern religions accept as a cure for the illusion of wanting to live at all. For others it is simply the consequence of ill-doing in an earlier existence. Although almsgiving is prescribed in many ethical traditions—the Muslim, among others—nowhere save in Jewry are the poor in some special way God's chosen ones, nowhere else is there a particularly explicit judgment—"Depart, ye cursed"—waiting to fall on those who neglect the miserable as Dives neglected Lazarus or who, like priest and Levite, "pass by on the other side." There is something in the Jewish prophetic tradition that stubbornly rejects any accommodation with the stratification of society, the wealth of the few, the misery of the many, the pride of the rich, the long-suffering of the poor, in short, the alienation and exploitation of man that comes into society with the division of labor, the property relations and hierarchies and privileges of post-tribal society.

What in other cultures tends to be seen as legitimate degree and order willed by the gods is usurpation and injustice to the unruly visionaries of Israel. No other culture shows this hunger for justice, this passionate belief in the right of every child of God to enjoy it. It is an egalitarian passion backed by a terrifying vision of Divine Judgment. However muffled its first appearance in Western Christianity, it has provided a lasting and irresistible dynamite of social change ever since.

Why this breakthrough to a new view of man and society should have occurred first not in the fabulous and wealthy Orient but in Western Europe where a total lack of precious metals, a miserable climate, and apparently meager resources of forests and fenlands seemed to create a remarkably unfavorable environment is a query that should remind us of the free, unpredictable, and unconditioned quality of history. It does not "abide our question." If out of a thousand young burghers of Stratford, it produces a Shakespeare, we may analyze the fact. We can never predict it. It is true that the phenomenon of Western Europe does resemble in some degree the previous miracle of Greece. Rude invading tribes brought in their vigor and freshness of response and met a much more sophisticated but weakened and decaying civilization—Doric Greeks fusing with Myceneans, the Norsemen overrunning the last of Rome. But the explanation takes us not much further for it cannot be generalized. Mongol invaders from the north had no such effect in Persia or India or China. The element of the unique, the unrepeatable and unpredictable remains to remind us once more that human affairs are not bound to iron laws of necessity and the spirit of creativity still "moveth where it listeth" to remake the face of earth.

The first hints of coming dynamism can be found in medieval Europe. The free citizen is foreshadowed in parliaments meeting to vote supplies as early as 1265. Divided authority at the top—in the war between pope and emperor—prevents the oppression of God and Caesar fused in a single authority. It also allows local rulers, cities, corporations to buy privileges in return for support, rather as today the dispute between Moscow and Peking has permitted Communist states in Eastern Europe to bargain for greater independence in return for their loyalty. The metaphysical roots of equality lie in the vision of the "Last Judgement," painted in thousands of parish churches, the great "Dooms" in which the shepherd and the laborer troop to Heaven while flames on the left hand engulf kings and barons and even a cardinal and a bishop or two as well. The rigor of scholastic debate sharpens the mental tools of later enquiry, orderly monastic life introduces the rhythm of year-round

work done to a timetable, the search for new technology and
energy appears in the fleet of windmills that suddenly take sail
all through Europe's maritime states. In short, a leaven was at
work even before the twin influences of Greece and Jewry
were traumatically increased by Renaissance and Reforma-
tion.

But from the sixteenth century onwards, the forces of dynamic change gather strength. The stream becomes a torrent.
In the volcano mouth of Western Europe, energy, innovation,
enquiry, confidence, violence boil up like molten lava flows
and begin pouring out all over the earth, incinerating old
ideals, overlaying old societies, creating a wholly new political
and economic landscape ultimately, no doubt, as fertile as rich
volcanic soil but at first harsh, bleak, unfamiliar, and often terrifying to those whose lives had been spent in peculiar un-
changing environments before the eruption.

In the four centuries that have passed, Western modes of
thought and action have taken over the planet. At the peak of
Western power—just after World War I—there were virtually
only three non-Western states, Japan, Siam, and Ethiopia, that
were not under one form or another of direct Western control.
But all without exception were having battered out of them
the concepts of millennial tribal or archaic culture. Man with
political rights and a claim to equality, man, the manipulator
and explorer of the material universe, man, actor and narrator
in a developing history fraught with Messianic hope and material progress—these were the new images the human race acquired of its own purpose and significance. The old conformi-
ties and fatalities could only fight a rearguard action. The

human experiment began to take shape as a common planetary exercise in dynamic and directed change.

But this flood of new thoughts, techniques, and visions did not obscure all the old landmarks. On the contrary, it took over a number of old institutions and poured new energy and purpose into them. One of these refashioned organisms we have briefly looked at already—the European nation-state. The old dynastic kingdom gave place to the new people's community gathering together the loyalty, the energy, the support of all the new increasingly equal citizens and giving them a common tongue to express their drives and demands. It became the formidable engine of world commerce and conquest. It became the forcing house of the new economics. As such, it was infinitely more formidable than any of the older, looser communities and potentially more lethal, too.

Another set of institutions to survive and be profoundly remolded by the new dynamism was the hierarchy of property, wealth, and rule—the property relations and class structures of Europe on the eve of the first breakthrough to modernization. And at this point we encounter yet another proof of underlying unity in the worldwide advance of Westernization. For over a century now, the process has not been a simple progression. The only way to describe it is in terms of a dialogue or debate or, in Marxist terms, the "dialectic."

Probably any dynamic system must proceed "dialectically," in other words, from error to correction and back again. Given the limits of human knowledge, the scope of any new experiment can only be tested by being pushed as far as it will go and, given the limits of human wisdom and good will, the point is likely to be too extreme. Man lives in need of opposites—of unity and diversity, of freedom and discipline, of self-assertion and altruism, of innovation and consolidation. It is almost impossible both to innovate and to keep a balance. So a dynamic society has trial and error built into it.

But the area covered by the debate must in a real sense express some elements of underlying unity—a common universe of discourse, if you like, a kind of intellectual magnetic field, an area of significant interplay between forces. There can, for example, be no genuine debate between racialists and democrats. Since racialists start by denying the fundamental dignity of all men, nothing fruitful can be learnt from exchanges with them. Fascism and freedom make up an equally sterile confrontation. Dominance by one nation on the grounds of its inherent superiority cannot be the premise of any constructive debate on world order. But there *can* be a genuine dialogue with an opponent who claims to share such basic Western beliefs as brotherhood, equality, the rights—and wrongs—of the poor, and the vision of mankind using its new tools of scientific thought and technological discovery to progress towards a juster and more peaceful world order.

This is not to say that there will be no Doublespeak and Doublethink in the debate. Annexation proclaimed as liberation, "people's democracies" with no free vote, peaceful coexistence covering highly unpeaceful subversion—we are all too familiar with the Communist liturgy of deceit. But the truth of their own claims is not the point. Even the language is a sort of tribute vice pays to virtue. The significance of the whole range of Marxist and semi-Marxist criticism in the last century has been its claim to attack and expose democratic society in terms of democracy's own values and pretensions. As a result, the impact of Western civilization on the rest of the world over the last hundred years has become increasingly complex, even ambiguous, since the same basic recipe—for innovation, for material advance, for progress, for equality—has been offered in violently competing terms. Yet as the competition and the debate have continued, little by little resemblances and concurrences appear to remind the outsider that free society and Communism spring from the same parent Western stock.

The original breakthrough to the modern society clearly belongs to the side of freedom in the Western tradition, to innovation, personal initative, and untrammeled experiment. Eighteenth-century entrepreneurs—the Wilkinsons, the Cokes, the Bridgewaters—could draw from confidence hundreds of years of constitutional rule in which their rights *vis à vis* the government had been guaranteed by law and their property protected against the violent sequestrations and expropriations normal under absolute monarchy. The new technology on which they drew had been the invention of free minds working in the spirit of free enquiry. Their actual operations—in investment and trade and foreign commerce—were felt to be liberating acts, as often as not in explicit rejection of the old mercantilist forms of state control. Without all this vigor and risk, this breakaway from old forms, this readiness to do without the privileges and monopolies of state support, enough momentum to blast the whole society into new methods of production is hardly conceivable. As we have seen, Adam Smith's dream of

the "great commercial republic" was essentially a generous and
liberal dream, a step forward from tyranny towards the liberation of mankind.

But Adam Smith himself had doubts about the behavior of
the new industrialists. He relied on the rigors of competition in
the free market to restrain their appetite for gain and their
readiness to use any method, including private monopoly, to
secure it. From the start, the new system contained dangerous
possibilities of abuse. It inherited the hierarchies and property relations of a society still emerging from the old unequal
feudal order. Property owners continued to receive the highest
rewards in the new society—even though fabulous productivity was multiplying the rewards out of all reason and the pattern of work which made such productivity possible sprang not
from any one individual's contribution but from a joint and indispensable partnership between the men who saved, the men
with enterprise, and the men who worked. Feudal patterns of
authority persisted in the factory with workers so subordinate
as to lose their human faces and become "hands."

Psychologically, too, these hangovers from an earlier social
order, when applied to the new and inconceivably dynamic
opportunities, produced inevitable perversions. In a society
where standards were set and privilege earned by immense
fortunes, it was easy to unleash a passion of avarice and speculation. In a society in which thousands of defenseless people
were set to work under unquestioned authority, it was easy to
encourage the brutality and bullying with which some natures
react in the presence of weakness. The England of the first
breakthrough—whether you study it, as did Engels, in official
Blue Books and Poor Law reports or read of it in the gloom

and squalor of Dickens' later novels—is a grim society in which the biblical sins which "cry to heaven for vengeance" —defrauding the worker of his hire and "grinding down the faces of the poor"—were virtually the foundation of the system.

Vengeance duly arrived in the person of Karl Marx. But he, too, derives his critique entirely from Western ideas and sources. We can leave on one side his claims to have discovered in dialectical materialism the scientific secret of man's history. It has the grandeur and excitement of a great work of art—the somber force of a Verdi opera, the flashing vision of Goethe's *Faust*. But like them, it belongs to the world of imagination, not of fact. It throws profound light on the nature of reality and widens man's vision. Nobody will ever think in quite the same way about history because of Marx. Property and class relations, the interaction between man's methods of producing wealth and devising institutions, the drive of material self-interest, the self-deception with which interests are proclaimed as ideals—all these factors will be weighed in making historical judgments as they never were in the days of the simple chronicling of battles and dynasties. But the Marxist vision of history, with its cosmic sweeps from slavery to feudalism to capitalism to communism, is not true in the sense that a scientific experiment or a plain record of dates and happenings is true. It cannot be tested. No predictions can be based on it. And it is contradicted by a large variety of facts.

The lasting significance of Marx lies elsewhere—in his criticism of contemporary Western capitalism in the name of Western ideals and in his reformulation, in modern terms, of the great Jewish-Western tradition of social justice—of the special care for the poor and the oppressed, the special judgment on the indifference of the rich. These aspects of his thought can be separated from the strict Marxism of dialectical materialism and indeed have been so separated as the rigid frame of historical interpretation has come to be seen as fanciful and irrelevant. But other root ideas in Marxism have been disseminated in the West over a whole spectrum of leftward-looking movements and parties. Together they provide the counterpoise to the equal diversity of groups and philosophies to be found on what, for want of a more accurate term, must be called the Right. But Marx gave the Left much of its force and bite and also provided the working philosophy of the first state—the Soviet Union—to be specifically founded on opposition to capitalism. The role of Marxism in the Western dialectic is thus central but not all-inclusive.

Marx led Left-wing criticism in attacking the old inherited property relations underlying the new capitalism. Possibly the uneven possessions and rewards of eighteenth-century Britain were a pre-condition of a first breakthrough to the new economy. Would a communal society or a community of yeoman farmers ever have produced enough savings or capital to finance the enormous installations of modern technology? Looking at the structure of tribal farming in Africa today, it seems unlikely. Nor were more or less egalitarian rural states such as Switzerland or Denmark pioneers of industrialization. But the fact remains that, given the wholly unexpected productivity of the new machines, fabulous gains were to be made from the surplus—or profits—earned over and above the costs of production in rent, interest, and wages. These profits flowed only to property owners, who thus came into possession of fantastically increased incomes. They too were the only ones to gain as the value of the property itself increased and share values rose. Yet the processes which produced these profits and capital gains were essentially cooperative. They depended as much on people offering labor as on people offering savings. But tradition placed the two types of people in the categories of masters and servants, not partners. Robert Owen's attempts to devise a different relationship in which a cooperative structure permitted a wider distribution of the gains succeeded in Britain only in certain forms of trade. In the first century of capitalism, during which Marx formulated his theories, it is broadly true to say that an inherited pattern of unequal ownership imposed even vaster inequalities on society by funneling virtually the whole surplus of the new system to a still highly restricted class.

Marx, as we have seen, did not believe this pattern would change. The "restricted class" was itself in charge of government and would ensure the continuance of its privileges—a forecast which incidentally has remained broadly true over many decades in certain societies of southern Europe and South America. Marx, therefore, believed the "bourgeois" state itself would have to be overthrown and a revolutionary government established, representative of all the people. This state would then take over the ownership of the means of production and thus ensure that the vast benefits of advancing technology would be shared more equally by all. Justice would be served. But so would the economy itself since a mass market would begin to take shape to absorb the rising output of the new machines. Only thus would the pretensions of capitalist society to freedom, progress, and abundance be achieved.

Freedom for the few to exploit the many, freedom for the managing class to progress at the expense of the majority, freedom for the property holders to acquire abundance out of the toil of the workers simply made nonsense of the word "freedom" and nonsense, too, of any ultimate hope of an expanding progressive economy.

But this rather dry outline of a rearrangement of state functions gives no sense of the real power behind the "anti-thesis" which Marx sought to set up against the "thesis" of early capitalism. His real force lies in the anger and outrage of the old Jewish prophets—of which he is the latest and also the most potent. If poverty is no more than the retribution for sin committed in an earlier existence, if it is only a useful pointer to the vanity of human existence, if it is no more than a sign of feebleness in an age when the fittest only survive—a view derived from debased Darwinism and very popular during the imperialist heyday of the 1880s—then, of course, the Marxist anathemata fall on indifferent ears among the wealthy and apathetic ears among the poor. But for men and women raised in the Christian tradition, his denunciations have an uncomfortably familiar ring. They have been heard before and from the West's own prophets and saints. Thus, though Marx formulated his philosophy in terms of atheistic materialism, his power is basically religious and makes no sense except in terms of a metaphysical belief in human freedom and responsibility. One cannot be angry in a scientific world. There the laws that govern human behavior allow no more free choice than the laws governing minerals or plants. There is no moral responsibility, hence no blame, hence no cause for anger. But Marx *is* angry. So are his followers. And much of the anger is derived from a religious judgment that men are free to act, and morally bound to do so, and that unredeemed poverty lies with a dreadful weight on the conscience of the rich.

Since Marx first formulated his philosophy, many forms of socialism have been evolved, some derived from it, some departing from it, but all concerned with his basic criticisms of the capitalist market economy. All agree on the need for a wider distribution of wealth and opportunity—"socialism is about equality" is one of the watchwords of Britain's Labour Party. Some of them still support the Marxist belief in public ownership as a means of making greater equality possible. But this belief takes far more varied forms today—varying from the complete ownership supported by some stalwarts on the Left of British Socialism to state supervision instead of ownership among Willy Brandt's German socialists. And this dilution of earlier dogmatism takes us back to the other side of the West's debate—the evolution of the market economies.

We need not repeat here the steps by which a larger measure of purchasing power and opportunity have been distributed to the mass of the people inside the Atlantic world and, as a result, have underpinned and enhanced the functioning of the economy. The point to underline is that forces which Marx dismissed as derivative and powerless—political conviction and religious faith—had a part in the evolution. Constitutional rights were extended to everyone, the vote did secure the poor majority important advances in income and opportunity, the well-to-do were taxed to spread more widely the wealth both from profits and capital gains, welfare and greater equality did come to be accepted as part of the "mainstream" of Western politics. The government could no longer be dismissed as the captive of a single class and the workers, through their parties and their unions, could directly affect political power. It is in recognition of this change that Italian Marxists led by Signor Nenni have been ready recently to take part in government and to justify their readiness by recognizing the inaccuracy of the old Marxist diagnosis of the state.

In these changes in the politics of the market economies the pressure of Socialist criticism and attack has been a potent factor. So was Christian reformism whether it appeared in the encyclicals of a Leo XIII or a Pius XI or in the moderate socialism of a line of Anglican bishops. Clearly, the freedom and social inventiveness of the Western tradition was in no way extinguished by the first breakthrough to the capitalist economy. When Lenin had to revise Marxism to allow for the bourgeois enrichment of Western workers, he was tacitly admitting that the first movement in the Western dialectic had come to an end.

Now we swing back to the Soviet experience. With the establishment of an officially Communist state in 1917, Marxism and all the variety of theories associated with it begin to lose their theoretical purity and to be tried out in actual practical governmental reality. One consequence has been a steady modification of confidence in the unlimited competence of public ownership, which in a curious way parallels decreased confidence in the virtues of all-regulating private property and enterprise. If the supporters of unlimited free enterprise overestimated men's ability to resist the temptations of enormous wealth and industrial autocracy, the Communists were just as naive about the likely moderation of men confronting unlimited political and bureaucratic power. Experience under Stalin and in the first years of imposed Communism in Eastern Europe suggested that the concentration of all economic power in the hands of public officials can lead to the blackest despotism. Those who had defended private economic power and decision-making as a hedge against tyranny were perhaps not after all the crafty, greedy conservatives their critics had made out.

Nor is it easy to move away from total bureaucratic control. The free societies of the Atlantic underwent varied political crises as they extended political and social opportunity to the mass of the people. But the process of extending to everyone a vivid experience of freedom and constitutional government formerly only enjoyed by the few has proved much less difficult than to introduce the first elements of freedom into a community hitherto run on totalitarian lines. Marx's claim that true freedom would be achieved by overthrowing the bourgeois state and substituting proletarian rule in the form of dictatorship has been violently disproved. The bourgeois state can extend its freedoms far more smoothly than any form of dictatorship knows how to modify its control.

In the functioning of the economy, too, the limitations of public ownership have begun to show up. It proved no magic wand to waft a nation through the rigors of primitive accumulation. On the contrary, by checking spontaneous saving in the countryside, by brutally collectivizing the land and returning no investment for the saving gouged out of the farms, Stalin made the transition much harder for millions of Russians and dealt Soviet agriculture a blow from which it has still not recovered.

As the system developed, the anomalies of state power and centralization persisted. The original strain of saving had eased, the industrial apparatus was in being. Now the time had come for a wider spread of its products. At this point the Soviet government began to encounter problems of distribution which, though different in kind from those of the market economy, were no less acute. The problem in the Atlantic world has been to get enough purchasing power to the consumers to buy the goods pouring out of the economy. The problem in the Soviet economy is to get enough goods, and also the kind of goods, to the consumers on which they are ready to spend their purchasing power. If the concentration of wealth in a few hands was an obstacle to an adequate flow of purchasing power in the market economies, the concentration of economic power in a central bureaucracy is just as much an obstacle to an adequate flow of the kind of goods the consumer really wants. Profits as the gauge of successful selling and efficient production are being rediscovered in the Soviet economy—just as planning as a possible means of sustaining and distributing income has had to be learnt by the market economies.

Clearly, this sustained debate between different versions of the modern society is not yet at an end. Pressure from the free communities on the continuing lack of political and artistic liberty in the Communist bloc will continue. The democracies are a challenge simply because they remain open, critical, and experimental. Equally, if the Communist system, decentralizing its decisions to local firms as in Russia and increasing the workers' sense of participation as in Yugoslavia produces a better version of industrial democracy, then it may offer a renewed challenge to industrial organization in the market economies. The need there to interest workers in problems of productivity, efficiency, and price and wage stability as a counter to possible inflation already seems to demand some institutional innovations such as more profit-sharing and more formal recognition of the workers' "managerial role" in the enterprise—Western Germany already has its experiments in joint-management, the *Mitbestimmungsrecht.* If these trends continue, it could be that in both systems the independent corporation will become the key institution of more democratic ownership and control.

One can think of other concurrences—the concern of both systems for the employment of less-talented citizens in a society calling out all the time for more skills, the deepening problems of monster cities in which men and machines try uneasily and dangerously to coexist, a certain underlying malaise about the whole fruits of affluence, the questioning about quality, the uncertainty whether materialism, however successful, is really enough. These are the preoccupations of relatively mature technological societies whose ideas of the good life are to a considerable degree drawn from a common civilization and whose methods of securing the good life are beginning to diverge less and less.

But Russia does not only face to the West. The relative *détente* with the West is only a part of its external relations. The combination it seeks of internal relaxation and external coexistence makes sense in the Western context. But there are other contexts and it is with them that the danger of ideological unbalance now lies.

In China, the tendency towards any easing of ideological rigidity is denounced as a betrayal of the revolution. The market is a symbol of bourgeois decadence and any pandering to the consumer is a disgraceful retreat from the puritan zeal of

Marx's original gospel. Strict centralized planning, the complete subordination of private whims to public needs must be maintained to strengthen and develop the people's economy. Thought must not diverge a hairsbreadth or permit even one unorthodox flower to bloom.

In foreign policy, the line is just as fierce. The arch enemy remains the exploiting, capitalist, bourgeois world which still grinds down the faces of the worldwide proletariat and squeezes its illicit profits out of the toil of the poor. To suggest a truce with this evil force is to betray the millennium. There can be no peace, no brotherhood, until these serpents have been expelled from mankind's potential Eden.

Moreover, the revolutionary techniques evolved by the Communists in China to crush the old Chinese nationalist regime—that of rural Communist guerillas encircling and stifling the "bourgeois" cities—is precisely adapted to the present stage of the world revolution. As Marshal Lin Piao, China's Minister of National Defense, recently put it: "Take the entire globe: if North America and Western Europe can be called 'cities of the world,' then Asia, Africa, and Latin America constitute the rural areas of the world. Since World War II the proletarian revolutionary movement has for various reasons been temporarily held back in North America and Western European capitalist countries while the revolutionary movement in Asia, Africa, and Latin America has been growing vigorously. *In a sense, the contemporary world revolution also presents a picture of encirclement of cities by rural areas.*"

In China's view, to relent, to call off this struggle, to settle for coexistence is a betrayal of the Marxist revolution and of the world's proletarian majority. The battle must continue and

if, as in Viet Nam, the "American imperialist aggressors" fight
to maintain their old rights of exploitation, then "the vast
ocean of several hundred million Chinese people in arms will
be more than enough to submerge American might."

Such is the scale of divergence within the supposedly unified ideology of Communism. But the rift is not really surprising. It fits into the successive stages of society's evolution towards an advanced, capital-intensive, modernized community.
Man's whole theory of exploitation was evolved, as we have
seen, during the early period of "primitive accumulation" in
Britain. The immense sums of capital needed to create the
bases of advanced technology—power, transport, city-build-
ing, industrial structures—demand that everyone should participate in the task of saving (or of postponing consumption)
and the country people who, by definition, are in a majority in
the pre-industrial phase, have to do most of the saving. Since
they are also, by definition, little above the subsistence level,
"primitive accumulation" can hit them, either as peasants or as
first-generation townspeople, the hardest blow in terms of
forced saving and marginal consumption—the poorer the
country, the harder the grind, the smaller the margin. It was
thus certain from the first that the already highly populated
countries of Asia would make the transition to the modern
economy with greater difficulty than the less-populated lands
of Europe and North America.

But, again as we have seen, once the apparatus of modern
technological production is in being, its fantastic productivity
begins to widen the margin again. In a sense, the tragedy for
Marx was that the full elaboration of his theory of the poor always getting poorer with the increase in technology coincided

in the 1860s with the poor getting richer just because of it. From that time onwards, the workers, white collar and blue collar, had enough to lose not to be revolutionary in the Marxist sense. When trouble struck—as it did, fiercely, in 1929— enough of them thought of themselves as "bourgeois" to make up the hysterically anti-Communist ranks of the Nazi party. Only one major society in the West failed to get past the phase of primitive accumulation without a Communist revolution— czarist Russia—and its backwardness stemmed in part from a semicolonial relationship with Western Europe, in part from patchy modernization and peasant unrest.

It was largely to explain the failure of Western society to become revolutionary according to the Marxist prediction that Lenin invented the theory that the Western system of colonialism and imperialism squeezed enough wealth out of the exploited "southern" continents to buy off and corrupt the workers of the West. They too, he argued, were now bourgeois but he slid over one valid reason for this change—their gains from the growing productivity and reformism of the West—and settled for an explanation that still had some smack of original Marxism about it—the exploitation of the poor nations by the rich imperialists.

Like Marx's earlier theory, there was some truth in the picture. The world economy is still biased towards the interests of the wealthy Atlantic community and the poor continents are, more or less, struggling with the acute problem of making the transition, via "primitive accumulation," to more tolerable standards and resources. But Lenin may also be, again like Marx, a little late. Not only have the European powers largely given up direct colonial control. They have embarked on programs of economic assistance which give some hope of reversing the old partially exploitative relationship. If, in the next twenty years, the proletarian continents follow the proletarian classes of the Atlantic world in a breakthrough to greater affluence and opportunity, then Lenin will need even more revision than Marx and the whole world will have embarked on the "revisionism" which the Chinese Communists so bitterly denounce.

But this transition still lies ahead in most continents. And they have acquired, since 1949, a new and formidable leader. The Chinese, unlike the Japanese, have failed to make the transition to modernity without a Communist revolution, and it is easy to see why. China, in the 1940s, was custom-made for Leninism. No Great Power in history has ever perhaps suffered such degrading humiliation at the hands of other nations. To go in half a century from the peak of self-confident civilization—Voltaire thought the Confucian system the model for Europe—to near-partition by the "outer barbarians" is a traumatic shock suffered by few. Add all the typical conditions of semi-modernization under external control—lopsided export sectors, stagnant farming, little industry, little credit, restricted, conservative education. Add the desperate challenge of securing the savings for the development from an overpopulated and bankrupt countryside. Then it is not difficult to see that China in the 1940s was like another and even more desperate Russia of 1917—a society torn from its moorings by the gale of Western ideas, trade, and investment and still unable to find its own way through the huge seas of early savings and investment. No one should underestimate—under these conditions—the attraction of a revolutionary solution which seems to explain every dilemma, puts the blame for every evil on an identifiable, external enemy, justifies every internal act of discipline, and continuously harnesses the desperate patriotism of sheer survival behind heroic rates of primitive accumulation.

This analysis suggests that one could reasonably describe Communism as "an infantile disease of early industrialism." Evolved as an explanation of the strains of the British breakthrough, it failed in the rapidly evolving West. Applied in Russia, it worked just for the years of greatest strain and is now disintegrating as society begins to edge up towards the problems of affluence. Taken up again in China, it dominates the present years of crisis and could spread to other societies similarly caught in the painful transition between old traditions and new hopes. But any society in which the transition is more or less complete no longer has much interest in the dogmatic certainties and solutions offered by Marxism-Leninism. Success feeds pragmatism and experience increases skepticism. The tendency at this stage is for developed technological societies—Western or Soviet—to converge in outlook and aspiration but also in unsolved problems and disappointed hopes.

It follows that the ideological unbalance in the world no longer runs primarily from West to East. The capitalism of the rich and the Communism of the rich are learning to speak a little of the same language. The ideological divide, like the divide of wealth, runs North and South, and it is here that ideology is still a major factor of division in a dangerous world. In a sense, we are back in the 1920s when the Soviet Union, as center of a new world faith, sought to lead and exacerbate the grievances of the world's dispossessed against their own governments. Today China sees itself as the new prophet of revolutionary change and clearly gives a very high priority to the task. How else can one explain the prime minister of some 700 million people visiting Africa three times in two years and proclaiming the prospects of revolution there to be excellent? One would have thought many more urgent tasks would have claimed him at home. Even at the height of Stalinist subversion, no Russian leader of such authority devoted comparable time to external "agitprop." Some Africans, it is true, cynically suggest that Chou En-lai's interest has something to do with China's vast surplus of manpower and Africa's relative emptiness. But the pattern of intense ideological activity extends beyond Africa and everywhere suggests the preliminaries to Marshal Lin Piao's grandiose schemes of "encirclement."

In a sense, this situation is less dangerous than the outlook in the 1920s. We now have the hindsight to see that the ideological fervor of Communism—its zeal, its discipline, its tough demands on its followers—may appeal to a dedicated few. But given even ordinary conditions of work and hope, the mass of citizens prefer a less heroic existence. The Soviet people, themselves, after showing unbelievable reserves of courage and fortitude under the Nazi onslaught, have found means, in spite of their one-party system, to impose on their leaders the search for better living standards and more personal elbowroom. There is nothing irresistible about Communism. On the contrary, it takes the violent upheavals of the first onslaught of modernization to make it even acceptable. If, therefore, in the next two decades, the "south" maintains a sense of momentum and confidence, we could see Communism dilute itself into a hundred splinter parties and movements and reduced to the

role—a useful role—of ginger group and voice of protest on
the leftward fringe of wider movements of social reform. Even
in their present poverty and uncertainty, Asian and African nations look at Chinese influences and intervention with a skep-
tical eye and—as in   Indonesia—counter it when they feel
their own national interests have been attacked.

A move to greater moderation is even possible in China provided it can follow the Soviet cycle from violence, despotism,
and massive forced saving on to successful modernization and
the emergence of "bourgeois" values as more and more people
find they have something to lose. Thus, if there is anything in
the theory that aggressive militant Communism is a phenomenon of the early stages of the breakthrough to modernity, then
the course of wisdom for a world that wants peace is almost
certainly to hasten with all possible means—of investment, of
trade, even of aid—the transition to a more "bourgeois" phase
in China's development. Once a truce is achieved there are
strong arguments for extending long-term reconstruction loans
to the industrious but capital-poor Chinese economy and
even stronger reasons for using all appropriate means to end
Chinese isolation. It is surely folly to leave in ignorant separateness a society whose whole historical tradition is that of the
"Middle Kingdom"—in other words, the sole significant occu-
pant of Middle Earth between heaven and hell. The "outer barbarians" today are, in China's view, bourgeois revisionists or
bourgeois exploiters all the way from Moscow to Washington
and back again. Only Peking has the purity, the heroism, the
faith to lead the world to the Marxist-Leninist millennium.
China therefore has the right to foment the "wars of national
liberation" needed to destroy the vestiges of bourgeois society. It is absolutely terrifying that a quarter of the human

race should live wrapped in such illusion. Far from pursuing any policy that feeds this exclusion, the outside world should be using every means to pour reality in upon them, to break down the walls, to expose the ideologies to great gales of fact. This is not to deny that daunting obstacles such as the status of Viet Nam or Formosa stand in the way, but all possible inventiveness needs to be mobilized to solve the longer term problems. They should not be lost to sight even though police actions continue.

Another source of hope lies in greater knowledge of the development process. Although no one can exactly predict when the processes of successful modernization will take hold, we know more about the conditions which make a breakthrough impossible or, on the other hand, more likely. Governments which will neither tax nor educate their people, countries in which vast underused estates impoverish the countryside and destroy the rural market for local manufacturers, presidents who buy factories as children buy toys, "soldier-statesmen" who divert scarce resources to imported military hardware, general indifference to galloping increases in population—all these represent, under different guises, the risk of stagnation.

Equally, expansive education, a population program, reasonable taxation to mobilize resources, far-reaching rural reorganization, industries built with proper regard for sales costs and profits can add up to a pattern of dynamic growth and, if the criticism is made that to equate such policies of modernization with the political and social needs of the people is to practice a sort of Marxism in reverse and argue that economic reorganization is the condition of political stability, in fact, the argument works in reverse. Only with a political will mobilized to transform the whole economy, cut out the special and vested interests and bring opportunities to all the people will the transformation occur. The appeal of Communism in the past has been precisely its claim to serve the majority and end the deadlocks of class rule. Its lack of appeal today is that after Stalinism, Mao's "Hundred Flowers" with their heads chopped off, and Fidel Castro's unattractive and rationed barrack room, the majority have to be pretty well desperate and without any alternative forms of political mobilization before they turn to it. Africa, still underpopulated and well fed, is making slow experiments with its own variants of "African socialism" which bear remarkable resemblances to the familiar idea of the mixed economy. Latin America, for all its strains, has begun a lively experiment in Christian democracy. Asia, under the dark shadow of war, looks more confused. But even there nations seem to have to be as ruined as was China in the forties before they turn to the extremes.

But now we come to the reasons for less confidence. Can we be sure that such ruin will be finally avoided? Is today only a lull? If we know more about the conditions of successful modernization, we must also know how far the mass of people in the developing world are from that threshold of promise. Indeed, we must realize the rampant speed with which in some areas conditions are getting catastrophically worse.

It is more difficult in many ways to make the breakthrough today than it was forty years ago. The surge of population has grown like a tidal wave and in continents such as Latin America where annual rates of growth have in places reached 3.5 percent a year, prospects of saving, prospects even of eating grow more dubious year by year. The surplus people pile up in the countryside and spill over into the mushrooming cities. But there the technologies of modern industrialism demand ever more capital, ever fewer people, so there is no work for them and the new industries may even be wiping out the old artisan trades and workshops that used to give some hope of employment. The tide of human misery at the base of society in the developing south is rising so fast—especially in Asia and Latin America and especially in the vast cities—that the time to achieve the beginnings of modernization under moderate leadership is ticking away, hour by hour, second by second, with each new migrant, with each new birth. And all the while more radical voices, offering the alternative of violence, become steadily more convincing as they lay the blame for present failures on past imperial rulers, now rich beyond belief, and denounce the Atlantic world, and even Russia too, as white, wealthy, exploitative, and indifferent.

One should not overlook the racial overtones. European domination has expressed itself all too often in racial contempt. In South Africa, it has been raised to a principle of government. In the immediate aftermath of colonialism, all too many yellow, brown, and black men remember comparable insults inflicted by the common overlord. The Chinese can offer especially relevant leadership here. They, a colored people, were humiliated, exploited, and nearly partitioned for a century, yet their revolutionary recovery has proved that, by using comparable techniques of mobilization, activity and subversion, the poor, ex-colonial and colored peoples can also "encircle" and crush the central white citadel. Perhaps not many people are listening now. But five years from now? With 100 million more mouths to feed? With farming still stagnant and unemployment filling the cities with despairing men? May not the audience be greater then?

In such conditions, knowledge of what should be done to hasten development in the "south" is only part of the problem. Where is the drive, the energy, the determination to give it the priority it desperately needs? This is the question that confronts the wealthy nations as they consider the potential ruin of half a world. Aid, trade, technical assistance, compensatory finance—in theory they add up to a technique of encouraging more rapid modernization, in theory, they could repeat in the world at large the end of proletarian misery more or less achieved inside the developed communities. But is the will there to mobilize them sufficiently and to do so in time?

We come now to the real ideological obstacle to a better functioning and more stable world. It is a fundamental mental block, so fundamental that millions upon millions of people do not even recognize it. The chief reason we cannot be sure that the Atlantic world will behave to the troubled "south" as the federal government behaves to Appalachia or the British government to Tyneside or France to its farmers is simply that the "south" is on the other side of national frontiers, whereas the other distressed areas or people lie inside. The difference is not in capacity or resources or needs or even techniques. It stems simply from our present national system which allows interests, investments, commerce, communication, propaganda to go all round the world but restricts obligation, loyalty, sustained policymaking, and responsibility to over a hundred centers of separate sovereignty. There is thus a fundamental disproportion between the worldwide web of interests and activities in which everyone is enmeshed and the narrow base of loyalty on which they build obligation, mediation, responsible citizenship, and mutual trust. Almost every major influence on a man's life today is international. His ultimate emotions and loyalties remain national. This is the gap through which our little world threatens to plunge to ruin.

The irrationality of divorcing loyalty and obligation from the real scale of interest and operation is frequently recognized in other contexts. Europeans are ready to be horrified when an Asian clerk or an African official puts the interests of his joint family or his tribal relatives before the safety or prosperity of the state. But the same European may well applaud a De Gaulle when he risks the prosperity of the Common Market in the name of French self-interest. Westerners curl their lip at the ridiculous pretensions of African tribalism and count among the blessings of Western colonialism that it rid Africa of "tribal war." Yet they look back on this century's infinitely more lethal wars between Teuton and Gaul in Europe as part of the normal political ordering of human society. They deplore war, of course, but they do not deplore the idea of total national sovereignty that made war inevitable.

Today we can feel little certainty that we shall repeat for the proletarian nations the transformation into self-confidence, self-help, and efficiency which was accomplished *inside* the nation for the proletarian classes. And the reason lies precisely in the differing context. You can do inside a nation what you cannot do between nations, and one of the reasons efficiency stops at the frontier is because at that point the mobilization of imagination and obligation ceases, too. Admittedly, it is very difficult for the citizen of a modern, well-established nation-state to extend beyond the nation his sense of moral purpose or social duty. The whole schooling of his imagination has occurred within the old tribal limits. But he should not think that such extensions are impossible. The seven kingdoms of Britain under the heptarchy of the Dark Ages was not the last word about British political organization. The single-village language-group of New Guinea is unlikely to be the last word there either. But neither the modern villager nor the ancient Mercian could imagine a wider loyalty. Perhaps some Frenchmen and some Britons cannot do so today. But if so, they are in the same condition of restricted imagination and feeling as the tribesman in New Guinea.

Today, inside our national communities, we recognize that the whole population has to be educated up to the limit of its talents. We recognize increasingly that some groups may need special help. We see that regions as well as people may be left behind in the course of dynamic development. We believe that, through tax and subsidy and rebate, more fortunate groups have to share their wealth with those who are not able to do so well and, although we do not expect immediate results—the *Mezzogiorno* after twelve years of effort still lags behind the Italian north—we have enough experience to know that, over a generation, the policies of retraining and investment will work and that the citizens whose standards have been raised will, in all probability, be contented and responsible members of a community that has fulfilled its obligations to them. In many areas in Europe, this policy could not have been followed successfully without some neglect of the old claustrophobic frontiers. Belgian miners in the declining coal fields of the Borinage have been retrained with funds from the

European Fund of the Common Market. In the whole Atlantic world, recovery itself would have been impossible after the war if America had not ignored national frontiers in the Marshall Plan.

Yet, such is the folly of human vanity and human reaction, it is in Europe, with General de Gaulle at its head, that a lead is now being given to abandon the post-nationalist attitudes and policies which worked brilliantly and go back to the nationalist self-assertions that made prewar disaster certain. Under this philosophy, clearly, sufficient and speedy investment in the developing south will not become the sustained obligation of a functioning world community. At the best, it will be a chancey search for clients, an uncertain reflection of national self-interest, a tap turned on or off according to irrelevant preoccupations with national diplomacy. At the worst, it will dry up as nationalist policies begin to undermine the prosperity which only international cooperation has made possible in the Atlantic world. In any case, although a considerable amount of aid has been given with nationalist purpose, it has often been the least efficacious—military aid, bribes to supposedly favorable leaders, dumping of unwanted materials, education in "the language and literature" of the donor goverment. What such self-regarding nationalist aid becomes only with difficulty is part of a sustained strategy for successful growth.

What are the chances of the human experiment rising above these nationalist contradictions? We have all too many grounds for pessimism. Since hominids have been dug up in Kenya with their sharpened weapons beside them, it seems clear that man from his origins has conspicuously failed to recognize a brother in fellow human beings who happened to stand in the way of his needs or intents. Or even if he does, he is ready for fratricide. Cain and Abel, after all, were brothers. To kill, maim, dispossess, and generally ruin a fellow member of the human race because he lives in "another part of the forest" is too ancient a reaction to be counted as anything but deep primeval instinct. All one can say is that as history has widened the area of community—from clan to city to state to continent —the frontiers across which violence is permissible have been thrust back. We avoid the head-hunting from village to village of Borneo or Papua. But when violence comes, it is all the more lethal and can now include the hydrogen bomb.

The instinct to kill strangers is thus an ancestral inheritance —part, if you like, of the original sin of the separate, self-regarding human ego. Transferred to the self-defense of the community, it acquires new vigor since many people will do for wider interests what they would hesitate to do simply for themselves. And of all communities yet invented, the modern nation-state seems to set new standards of calculated ferocity. This is because, as Professor Toynbee has pointed out, democracy and modern technology involve everyone's drives and everyone's interests. So the nation-state, based on both, is a potential juggernaut of power and will. The dynastic empires floated on top of the people's ordinary lives. The villagers ran their own communal affairs and lived by their own subsistence economies. War and conquest ebbed and flowed largely without their consent or concern. But the modern nation-state brings back in a sense the unity and involvement of the tribe. Everyone's livelihood depends on the national economy. Everyone's opinion must be consulted in forming the national consensus and one easy way of creating unity in a large, potentially diverse group is clearly to do so in rivalry and hatred for rival groups. French and British nationalism was ground to a fine edge by hundreds of years of hostility. This extraordinary concentration of civic and personal commitment and economic self-interest has put an irresistibly violent emotional charge behind the institution of the nation-state. In the United States a revolution "dedicated to a proposition" of liberty and equality has produced the American nation. In the Union of Soviet Socialist Republics, the old lineaments of Holy Russia have reappeared beneath the mask of Marxist revolution. Neither the liberal revolution of democracy nor the radical revolution of Communism has much modified the master-institution of modern Western civilization—the absolute, uncompromisingly sovereign nation-state.

Must we then conclude that the present disproportion between man's physical and scientific environment and his political means of dealing with it is destined to continue, with all the appalling risks it entails, of deadlock and conflict and destruction? That is the risk, certainly. I will confess that I myself never hear the baroque eloquence of President de Gaulle expanding on the claims and grandeurs of *la patrie* without seeing hundreds of scarecrow bodies pinned against the barbed wire of the front-line trench. Yet it is possible that pessimism underestimates the realism and inventiveness of the human community. If there were no capacity to change and adapt, would we have advanced beyond the tribe? Loyalties have steadily emerged at a higher level as the scale of organized human activities has increased. The age of the rocket and the spacecraft already has a few post-national experiments and institutions on which to base a new planetary loyalty. The United

Nations is an embryo of world order with a hint of a police force and a sketch of a judiciary, the International Monetary Fund could foreshadow a World Reserve Bank, the U.N. Food and Agriculture Organization a Ministry of Agriculture, the World Health Organization a Ministry of Health. No doubt this is, like some of the Doublespeak of Marxism, the tribute of unrepentent sovereignty to its own obsolescence. But the tribute is significant after all. We have some kind of world institutions for the first time.

What they lack is the loyalty in ultimate decisions which at present goes no further than the national level of government. And this is not a matter of institutions—which, in a sense, we have. It is a matter of ideology. It is a matter of belief and we may wonder whether, anywhere, in our angry, divided and competing world, there is any source of strength sufficient to underpin a wider loyalty.

Yet there is first of all the force of reason. When the astronauts spin through more than a dozen sunrises and sunsets in a single day and night; when the whole globe lies below them with California one minute and Japan the next; when, as they return from space, they feel spontaneously, with the first Soviet spaceman: "How beautiful it is, *our* earth"; it is inconceivable that no modification of consciousness or imagination occurs, no sense that quarrels are meaningless before the majestic yet vulnerable reality of a single planet carrying a single human species through infinite space. In the decades ahead, more distant journeys will begin. They will appeal to the bravest, coolest, most adventurous minds. These pioneers will surely not tolerate the petty quarrels which could destroy their launching pad and their haven of return. No one expects a wider citizenship from the bushmen living in intimate isolated daily contact with the beasts and springs of the barren Kalahari Desert. But what may we not expect from men whose habitat is increasingly the heavens and who learn to see the earth as, today, we see the moon? On a smaller scale, Europe escaped from the claustrophobia of the Middle Ages after the Black Death when Columbus made landfall in a new continent. But what lies ahead is a landfall in a new planet and a dimension added to the human adventure possibly as vast and as unpredictable as the amoeba's first stirring in the warm salt waters of the primal earth. Changes on this stupendous scale will not leave the human imagination unmoved. They cannot fail to change the context and significance of petty terrestrial squabbles.

Another source of vision is surely the scientific temper. No tests yet made reveal anything but a single identifiable human species, conditioned, no doubt, by different cultures and environments but in substance, one and indivisible. Nor is it simply a question of scientific witness to the underlying unity of the human race. The scientist studies other unities and has a universal language. Assemblies of experts and scholars already transcend national boundaries since their interests reach, by definition, beyond the limitations of place. Quicker transport and communication makes contact across frontiers a matter of course and helps to build up communities of like-minded men and women for whom the discipline, the truth, the adventure of their field of learning far outweigh the differences of language or politics which their national origins impose.

And even in faith itself, which has divided the world so bitterly, there is evidence of a new concern for unity. The ecumenical movement is above all an attempt to reach beyond the differences of the past in order to encounter the reality of a common human experience, a sense of brotherhood, if the term has not been overused, a discovery of what unites rather than divides the communities of the world. The Pope himself has visited the United Nations to underline the fact that for the first time in the human record all the peoples of the world share in some measure a common jurisdiction. This is, he said, "a new history," a new age in which the nations must transcend the pride and egoism and collective self-love which hold them apart, and form instead the habits and institutions of a common life. After all, one of the fundamental moral insights of the Western culture which has now swept over the whole globe is that, against all historical evidence, mankind is not a group of warring tribes, but a single, equal and fraternal community. Hitherto, distances have held men apart. Scarcity has driven them to competition and enmity. It has required great vision, great holiness, great wisdom to keep alive and vivid the sense of the unity of man. It is precisely the saints, the poets, the philosophers, and the great men of science who have borne witness to the underlying unity which daily life has denied. But now the distances are abolished. It is at least possible that our new technological resources, properly deployed, will conquer ancient shortage. Can we not at such a time realize the moral unity of our human experience and make it the basis of a patriotism for the world itself?

Index